Edisto Island

Edisto Island

A NOVEL

NANCY RHYNE.

NONSUCH

Published by Nonsuch Publishing
An Imprint of The History Press
Charleston, SC 29403
www.historypress.net

Cover painting by Alan C. Brooks.
First published 2006

Manufactured in the United Kingdom

ISBN 1.59629.179.6

Library of Congress Cataloging-in-Publication Data

Rhyne, Nancy, 1926-
  Edisto Island : a novel / Nancy Rhyne.
    p. cm.
  ISBN 1-59629-179-6 (alk. paper)
  1. Edisto Island (S.C.)--Fiction. I. Title.
  PS3568.H95E35 2006
  813'.6--dc22

                        2006023898

Notice: The information in this book is true and complete to the best of our knowledge. It is offered without guarantee on the part of the author or The History Press. The author and The History Press disclaim all liability in connection with the use of this book.

This book is a work of fiction. No living counterpart to any of the characters exists.

To know is nothing at all;
To imagine is everything.

—Anatole France

Preface

*B*enjamin Bodicott came to life for me through the pages of two WPA field reports I read while doing research in August 2005 at the South Caroliniana Library at the University of South Carolina in Columbia. The man featured in those stories frequently spoke in polysyllables. In order to explore the options of using that voice in a story, I made copies of the reports and took them home to study. My copies of the field reports became blotted all over as I decided, while sipping numerous cups of coffee, on the words I would use in the dialogue of this novel. One of the WPA reports on this South Carolinian was entitled "A Particular Genius," and revealed that he was a snappy dresser and a super salesman for his day and time. In real life as well as in this novel, he chose to sell fertilizer in an area where farmers planted cotton. But the thing that intrigued me most about him was that although he didn't have to skimp, he seemed to adhere to the belief that man's greatest treasure is to live on a little and be contented. That moral attitude appealed to me, and I believed it was a good way to define the man's character. Lord Byron wrote: "'Tis strange—but true; for truth is always strange; Stranger than fiction." Daniel Webster said, "There is nothing so powerful as truth—and often nothing so strange."

This book would not have been accomplished had I not found at the Caroliniana Library the stories of that peculiar genius, and I couldn't have written it without the assistance of the staff of librarians at the Caroliniana Library, my computer technician Bruce England and my very able editor, Julie Foster. Kudos to Sid Rhyne, who remains supportive and encouraging as I forge ahead with the work I love.

*T*he sight of what was known as the Old Seabrook Mansion had a palpable design upon us. Benjamin uttered, "Beauty. Quality."

I added, "Mysteries and stories that touch the soul."

Chapter One

*I*t wasn't like me to fall head over heels with an aristocrat, let alone Mr. Bodicott. As I sat on the porch, my meditation threw back images of his flashing blue eyes and floating hair. He was splendidly clothed in his usual corduroy jacket, tan trousers, plaid shirt and leather boots, as near a Rhett Butler as one could get. He looked the same every time I saw him in his store—the Feed and Seed they called it. Mostly it was a fertilizer business. Some of the island people had gardens and other folks, like us, planted large fields of cotton. Daddy lived and died by fertilizing his fields of cotton. From the 1790s until now, Edisto Island has been known for its cultivation, harvesting and sale of as fine a product of sea-island cotton as there is in the world.

I had heard Mr. Bodicott's name mentioned often during the several years he had lived on Edisto Island. The fertilizer he sold to the planters was the main reason. He didn't socialize with the island residents because there were no island organizations. The islanders met at church on Sunday and swapped the news of how their crops were growing and if anyone had come down sick. They liked each other, would do anything to help in an emergency, but they didn't socialize. I had no idea how much money Mr. Bodicott had, if or where he had gone to college or where he came from, let alone why he chose to live on Edisto Island, but every time I saw him a tingle went up my spine. If I gave in to it, the tingle became a shiver.

Mr. Bodicott was a blue blood and anybody could see that. He walked a little straighter than other men and spoke in a smooth, well-modulated voice. Poise was his very essence, and tact and consideration were the secret of his success on Edisto Island. He would have been the man who when inventing gloves would have remembered to put the warm furry cloth on the inside. His pearly whites were clean and even, obviously well tended, but the words that passed through them were the talk of Edisto. He didn't speak very much but when he did, everybody listened. They were obsessed with his ten-dollar words, not to mention the architecture of his sentences. Almost nobody knew exactly what he said but they were careful not to let Mr. Bodicott know that they didn't get the gist of his words. I had heard him utter only a few sentences and looked forward to one of his impromptu speeches. Daddy said Mr. Bodicott didn't believe in gaudy blabbing. He said he reckoned that, anyway, when Mr. Bodicott talked he probably didn't intend for the folks to figure out just what he was saying. I asked Daddy how come that was so and he allowed it was Mr. Bodicott's nature. Mr. Bodicott used three-, four- and five-syllable words.

Daddy believed it would take a philosopher to define the words the fertilizer merchant spit out. A lot of phrases were winnowed out in regular conversation but when he got down to real talk he pronounced all the syllables and you knew there was a lot going on in his head. You could tell it by that osprey look in his blue eyes. As I thought about it, he probably wouldn't cast an eye toward me, but then again, he didn't have that many people to talk to. Besides, he wasn't that much older than I was. Daddy said Mr. Bodicott was about twenty-two when he bought the land where he built the Feed and Seed. That was in 1952, four years ago. Give or take a little, he was about four years older than I was, and that was how it should be. I didn't have much going for me, like a special talent or anything, but I was about to undertake a conscious endeavor that would elevate my life.

When the day came that Daddy said, "Whaley, get in the car. We're going to Charleston to buy you a piano," I could hardly believe it. He went on, "When I was growing up on the plantation, my sisters took music lessons from a neighbor lady. Lill was right talented. She learned to play the 'Moonlight Sonata.' Who knows? You might take after Lill and learn fast." Charlotte Ann Kell, whose father owned a herd of dairy cows on the island, taught music. Daddy must have thought about Charlotte Ann because there was nobody else on the island who could play the piano.

When we entered the music store in Charleston, Daddy took off real fast toward the grands. I gazed at the uprights. Daddy couldn't pay for a grand and I knew it.

"What kind of wood is this?" Daddy asked the salesman as he rested his hand on the music stand.

"Cherry."

The salesman sat on the bench and played a few notes of "Tea for Two." The haunting melody shuttled me right over to them.

Daddy eyed a small instrument sitting beside the music stand. "What's this?"

The salesman explained, "That's a metronome. It's of cherry as well. A perfect match for the piano. A metronome is a timer that helps piano students count the time allotted to the notes."

"How much is it?" Daddy asked. "*The piano.* How much will you take for it?"

"This piano is a Baldwin, the best." The man's nimble fingers zipped up and down the keys. "Four hundred dollars."

"Does that include the metronome?"

The man hit an impressive chord. "I'll throw it in if you buy the piano."

My heart was thumping. Why in the world would Daddy pay four hundred dollars for a piano? He had finally gotten me through Coker College and I knew that no person in our circle of acquaintances had four hundred dollars to plunk down on a grand piano.

"What is your name?" Daddy asked the salesman.

"DeShazo. I'm the owner of this place, DeShazo's Piano Emporium."

Daddy looked at him quizzically. I wondered if Daddy was thinking what an unusual name DeShazo was, or could it be that he was actually contemplating buying the piano?

"Mr. DeShazo, if I buy this piano for my daughter, will you personally deliver it to Edisto Island?"

"You can take my word," the man answered as he got up.

Daddy asked him if he would play for us, and Mr. DeShazo said he would play as long as there were people to listen. Daddy wrote a check and handed it to him just like he passed out four-hundred-dollar checks every day. Mr. DeShazo gazed at the check and said he would deliver the piano before dark the following day.

Could it be real? I was thinking. Daddy's motto always had been that a person is rich in proportion to the things he can live without. I could live quite comfortably without the Baldwin grand, but I had a hunch that Daddy wanted to live in a home filled with music. Mother didn't care that much about it, but I did. Daddy and I. *Two of a kind.*

On the way home Daddy said he needed a hoe handle. He casually mentioned that we would stop at the Feed and Seed. I

14

didn't comment on that. Daddy had done one remarkable thing under the sun on that day and I couldn't expect another huge event, such as seeing Mr. Bodicott. I wondered, though, how in the world Daddy had enough money left to buy a hoe handle. Four hundred dollars must have been more money than he had dealt with in his entire life, but having the money to pay for the hoe handle was the least of my thoughts just then. With the palms of my hands I smoothed my skirt and patted my hair. Daddy didn't say anything and I hoped he hadn't noticed.

Mr. Bodicott was sitting in a rocking chair on the porch of the store when Daddy pulled into the yard. The proprietor got up. He straightened his back and ran his fingers through his curly brown hair. Oh my mercy, I was getting that tingle.

I jumped out of the car so fast Daddy didn't have time to slow me down. "Mr. Bodicott, I want to invite you to come to our house tomorrow afternoon. Later, you know, after you close the store. What time do you close the store?"

"About sundown." He looked bewildered but his lips moved into a smile. Daddy tried to take over the conversation by mentioning the hoe handle, but I jumped right in and said, "Daddy bought me a Baldwin grand today, a really *grand* piano." I realized I was flustered and should hush my mouth right then but I kept going. "Mr. DeShazo is to deliver it tomorrow afternoon before dark, and we're inviting all the people on the island to come to our house and hear him play the piano."

Daddy looked at me as though I had turned ghostly. I quickly marched inside the store and took a deep breath. They came in and Mr. Bodicott produced the hoe handle. I moved closer to them. On the spur of the moment Daddy asked for two fifty-pound bags of fertilizer and Mr. Bodicott told him he would load it from

15

the outside of the building. Daddy removed his checkbook from a pocket and carefully filled in the amount and signed his name. Mr. Bodicott watched every movement of Daddy's hand. I had long believed that Daddy had the prettiest handwriting of anyone I knew. The expression on Mr. Bodicott's face told me he felt the same way. Daddy handed the man his check and Mr. Bodicott studied it, looking intently like a great seaman gazing into the distant horizon. Finally he pulled his eyes away from the check and produced two pieces of clean, white paper. He handed one to Daddy. "Write my name," he said.

"Your name? Why should I write your name?" Daddy inquired.

"Benjamin Bodicott."

Daddy took his pen and wrote in his most beguiling manner *Benjamin Bodicott*.

Mr. Bodicott's countenance changed to the divine. His teeth were crystal, shining brightly. He pushed the other piece of paper to Daddy. "Write 'Bodicott's Feed and Seed.'"

Daddy asked no questions this time but wrote the name of the company in his flourishing script. Mr. Bodicott slipped the papers into the drawer with the money. I noticed his hands. They were clean and pure, firm and white. I put my own hands on the counter. They didn't compare favorably with his and I quickly moved them away. Mr. Bodicott noticed the quick withdrawal of my hands. His face was serene. With a quick glance my way, he uttered one word: "Tomorrow."

I returned to the car and tried to compose myself. I couldn't help wondering if Mr. Bodicott would come to our house tomorrow. Daddy propped the hoe handle against the backseat of the Plymouth and slid under the steering wheel. Mr. Bodicott loaded the heavy sacks of fertilizer into the trunk. When the car was turned onto the island road I ventured to bring up Mr. Bodicott's name, hoping Daddy would say whether or not he believed he would attend the event tomorrow. He didn't say anything.

"Mr. Bodicott is a nice man," I went on.

Daddy went further. "He has a gentle voice and manner. His modesty never seems to fail him. He's a refined boy, which is more than I can say for a lot of the people we know. Some of the folks of this new generation don't know how to spell grace and modesty, much less apply it." After a moment he added, "I just can't figure out why he asked me to write his name and the name of his business."

"I wondered about that. You handled it nicely."

"What else could I do?"

"Perhaps it was nothing more than your penmanship, which is wonderful." My mind rushed on to the event of the next day. Oh, the agony of wondering what would happen was almost too much to bear. One thing was for sure: I had told Mr. Bodicott that we were inviting all the people on the island to hear Mr. DeShazo play the Baldwin grand, and it was up to me to see that we did it.

When Daddy talked about grace and modesty it brought the thought of my mother to mind. There was no one in the world more modest than my mother, Emma McLeod. She rarely left the house except to go to church. She always assumed that the home was her obligation. When she needed groceries she made a list and Daddy went to the little store near the ocean. Mother made biscuits three times each day, for breakfast, dinner and supper. My clothes and those of my sister, Jonny, were handmade by her and she hand-washed everything. Her knuckles were red, always, from using the washboard. She spent much of the summers standing by a blazing stove, canning tomatoes and beans for winter use. In the cold of winter, she carried the scuttle to the woodshed and filled it with coal for fireplaces in three rooms. It was her burden, and she wore it proudly and quietly. One thing worked in her favor, though. Carrying out all her chores kept her as thin as barbed wire. She was rather tall and although she sewed her clothes, they were a perfect fit for her slim body. She went to the beauty shop twice a year for a permanent. Daddy always drove her wherever she went because she never learned to drive. When she came out of the beauty shop, with her hair short and stylish, Daddy never failed to look at her eagerly and call her "Wallis," the name of the fashionable woman who had married England's King Edward VIII. Mother liked the attention she received and loved being called "Wallis." She responded by rolling her eyes and wiggling her hips a little. In looks she would have compared favorably to Wallis Simpson, the Duchess of Windsor, had she had her share of wealth and opportunities. For Mother, work brought its own relief. She was a woman who had very little time for folly or play. That's the way it had been her entire life. Her father had been a sharecropper and moved his family from farm to farm. Mother was the cook for all of that family.

Daddy, on the other hand, had been raised on the plantation. His sisters had college educations, taught school and played the piano. Lill had married and moved to New York. She knew everything about opera. Each year when she visited us on Edisto Island, while Mother cooked for her and kept her in cool, clean bedclothes, Lill told us stories about Lily Pons, Grace Moore and other opera singers. One night we all were seated at the dining room table. Lill and her husband William talked about some of the famous divas and prima donnas they had seen at the Metropolitan Opera House and the theatre. Lauritz Melchior was mentioned, and Jeannette McDonald. I interrupted, "I wish I had a famous name, something like Pons or Melchior or Eddy." Lill and William were not a bit guarded in the way they corrected me when they blurted, "You *make* the name. The name does not make you famous." I still wanted to be like the people they admired, folks who loved music, played the piano, sang the arias, got an education.

My sister was different from me. Of the two of us, Jonny was the pretty one. Her Christian name was Emmajohn, a combination of our parents' names, but we called her Jonny. She was at Coker College, my alma mater. She had never been a very good student and had no interest in music. She majored in education, but I didn't know what sort of job she would end up with and I didn't know what kind I would have. I hadn't given any attention as yet to going out and finding my niche. Six months ago, when I returned to the island from Coker, I just wanted to crawl along like a loggerhead turtle for a while and enjoy the starry skies of the island. But now all I wanted was for Mr. Bodicott to come to our house tomorrow. Thinking of that, I was reminded that I had very little time to deliver the invitations.

Daddy unloaded his items and I rushed to Mother with the news of the Baldwin grand. My words bubbled out like an uncorked bottle of champagne. Mother smiled and went calmly about her affairs. She perked up a little when I told her that everyone on the island would be invited to our house tomorrow for a recital. She said she would sweep the living room and bake some cookies for the children.

I drove to each of the homes on the island, the mansions and the caretakers' cottages, urging everyone to come to the musical event. My enthusiasm spread and some of the islanders said they would be there. It wasn't often they had the opportunity to hear music played on a Baldwin grand. Driving back home, my thoughts submitted themselves to my soul: *Oh, what if? What if Daddy had not had the four hundred dollars with which to pay Mr. DeShazo for the piano? What if Mr. Bodicott actually comes to our house tomorrow? What if I really can learn to play the piano, pieces such as Lill talked about?* One of the pieces came to mind: Rachmaninoff's "Prelude."

Chapter Two

The islanders strolled into the yard two-by-two, entire families and gangs of children, but there was only one I was looking for. Oh my mercy, if I possessed the world I'd give all of it to have him show up. While deep in thought over the islanders' arrival I noticed a large truck in the distance, a vehicle much like the one used to deliver goods from the Feed and Seed. I prayed, *Let it be Mr. Bodicott*. It wasn't Mr. Bodicott but Mr. DeShazo, delivering the Baldwin grand. Just then Mother called to remind me that after the piano had been placed, the women and children would be invited into the living room. The men could stand outside, near the windows.

Spring was a short season at Edisto Island. It could be moderately cool one day and ninety-five degrees the next, and it would stay that way from that day until fall. That is what happened on the evening the piano was delivered. Some of the children were hot and restless. I tried to cheer them with promises of what was to come.

Daddy helped Mr. DeShazo unload the piano from the bed of his truck. The instrument was covered in a blanket. I was dying to see it, but it was still covered when it was carried to the front porch. Daddy and Mr. DeShazo became involved in a quiet conversation. No one seemed to know what the holdup was, but everyone was waiting for something to happen. Finally, Mr. DeShazo removed the blanket and announced that the legs of the instrument would have to be removed in order to get the piano through the front door. He went to his truck and brought back a toolbox. He and Daddy got busy and the legs were removed in a jiffy. They gingerly carried the main part of the piano into the living room. Daddy went back to the porch for the legs and held them in place while Mr. DeShazo screwed them back on. The next question that arose was where the piano would best fit in the room. They discussed moving the sofa and two chairs to another location and placing the piano in a corner. A couple of other possibilities were discussed and they came back to the original decision. When the piano was in the corner and the sofa and chairs in their new location, the women and children quietly moved closer to the piano. Mother and Daddy stood with them. The Middleton twins, Callie and Sallie, with whom I had attended school, stood in the dining room doorway. As usual, they were wearing matching outfits—this time blue gingham print sundresses with white cardigans. This had been their custom since they were young girls. I thought it slightly ridiculous and was glad Jonny had never had such a notion as to dress like me. I looked over at the twins and gave a small smile. They were clearly envious.

I stepped over to the window and glanced out. The men were in short-sleeve shirts. Some of them smoked as they quietly gazed at the window. And then I saw Mr. Bodicott. He had on summer slacks with a sharp crease and his short-sleeve shirt was crisp and starched. As usual, he was the most immaculate man in the group. He stood to one side of the other guests. Mr. DeShazo made another trip to his truck and returned with the metronome, which he placed in its location by the music stand. He sat down on the piano bench and said, "Ready for a concert?"

"You bet!" one of the men called through the window.

"What kind of music do you prefer?'

No one answered. I picked up the slack and asked him if he could play Alexander's "Ragtime Band." It was a popular piece with my friends. He didn't answer but went right into the march, letting his long, thin fingers fly to the highest notes and back to the center of the keyboard. It was so engaging, so *moving*, I couldn't keep still. I snapped my fingers and mouthed the words as he played. Could I ever play like that? When the piece ended he went straight into "Sweet Sue," and then changed the tempo and played the lilting "Blue Danube." The women swayed with the music and their faces revealed their feelings that were soaring in the grandeur of the sounds coming from the piano. Mr. DeShazo allowed his fingers to dance across the keys and began George Gershwin's haunting piece "Summertime." Most of the women knew that one because Mr. Gershwin had lived at Folly Beach when he composed it. It was said he and his cousin attended an AME church near Kiawah Island and heard a lyric soprano sing a similar song in a high minor key. Mr. Gershwin went right home to Arctic Avenue and wrote the song that very night. I thought that nothing else would compare to "Summertime," but suddenly I heard my favorite piece in the whole world, "Clair de lune." I had never heard that piece played except at weddings. I looked outside at Mr. Bodicott, who seemed to be in a sort of trance, facing the window. His head was moving to the dreamy beat and his abundant hair, now burnished golden by the sun, appeared similar to a floating bracelet. Mr. DeShazo, I believed, came to the conclusion that he would bring everybody back to reality by hammering the "Battle Hymn of the Republic." His repertoire ended with "Auld Lang Syne." The back of his shirt was wet with perspiration. Mr. DeShazo said his good-byes and left rather quickly.

If my thoughts had not settled on Mr. Bodicott, I would have been thinking of Charlotte Ann Kell and my music instruction. I surely would go to visit her tomorrow to try to set up some lessons. But rather than make such plans, I flew outside and asked Mr. Bodicott to come inside and view the instrument. He came in, and a few of the men accompanied him. They asked Daddy some questions about the piano and some of the women asked me if I planned to take piano lessons. "Oh, yes," I almost squealed, "Very soon."

There were a few remarks about one of the women on Edisto who had taken sick, and then the people began to leave. They were both exhilarated by the music and wilted from the heat. Mr. Bodicott was the last to go. The heat hadn't withered him in the least. I asked him if ever he had heard the history of Edisto Island. He shook his head to indicate he had not. I told him I would like to take him on a tour, and he said he did not open his store on Sunday and that would be a good day for it. That was the way it ended. He didn't say whether or not he would come for me on Sunday. He was very polite, thanking Mother and Daddy for the evening of beautiful music, not saying much, just bowing his head and smiling. I had begun to wonder about the manner of Mr. Bodicott's speech that Daddy and the other people talked about. When would I hear such a speech?

When the house was quiet I sat down at the piano and let my fingers skim over the keyboard. The tone was heavenly but I needed to take lessons. I could hardly wait to talk with Charlotte Ann Kell.

Chapter Three

I awoke wondering when I had last visited the Kells' dairy farm. I had been there once or twice and looked forward to going again. Huge oak trees shaded the front yard, and the house was painted white. That's about all I could remember. At breakfast I asked Daddy if I could take the Plymouth. He said he planned to use the pickup that day. I pulled on a skirt and white shirt and slid my feet into saddle oxfords. In the car I sang Alexander's "Ragtime Band." "Oh, come along…oh, come along…" I didn't know anyone else who could play the piano in the manner of Mr. DeShazo except Charlotte Ann. She had borne her talent from day one. She played the piano at the Church of the Tides on Sundays, and there wasn't a school event that she didn't play for. Everybody knew her. The only thing that worried me was that she might be getting married soon, and she might move away. She had been in love with a pharmacist in Charleston, or so I had been told. If she left Edisto Island I would just have to drive to Charleston—there was no way I would miss out on taking piano lessons from Charlotte Ann Kell. I was thinking so hard and was going on so that I almost missed the graveled driveway that led to a parking area. The house was nearly concealed in trees and high, bushy shrubbery. Two narrow brick walkways led through the foliage. I didn't know which one to follow. Just then Mrs. Kell showed up.

"My, I'm pleased to see you, Whaley. I suppose you're here to talk with Charlotte Ann. She's teaching right now."

I followed Mrs. Kell as she made her way through the shrubbery to a patio. I sat down in one of the chairs that surrounded a small table. A basket of fresh grapes was on the table. "I hear you have a splendid piano, a Baldwin grand."

I must have beamed like the sun that was almost blinding my eyes. "It is very nice. I still can't believe it's ours." I removed a handkerchief from my purse and pressed it against my damp forehead.

Mrs. Kell got up. "I'll bring you a glass of chocolate milk."

I thought how very nice she was. Chocolate milk was something I didn't have often. As I thought about it, running a dairy and all, I supposed the Kells had all kinds of milk. When she came back and set a tray with a glass of chocolate milk on the table I asked Mrs. Kell if she thought Charlotte Ann would give me music lessons. She said of course her daughter would teach me to play the piano. I nearly jumped out of my skin. While brushing off the table with a napkin, she went on, "You know, Charlotte Ann was awarded a scholarship to Duke, but she chose Converse because of the music program. She always wanted to have the benefit of that program and it was good for her."

I drank the milk quickly and set the glass on the table. Something was coming to mind, something about a concert. Suddenly I remembered that the Church of the Tides was getting a new pipe organ, and I'd heard that Charlotte Ann would play it in concert on a Saturday night. There was no question that I would be present for that event.

The grapes glistened in a ray of sun and their cool skin tempted me. I selected a large one and slowly laid it on the tip of my tongue, feeling exhilarated to be so well accepted at the Kell home. I thought of Delilah and her grape in a recent movie about Sampson and Delilah. The purple grape lay on Delilah's tongue for a second before the rich juice burst on her palate as it had done on mine. I was Delilah, discovering glory in such a simple act as eating a grape while I waited for the music teacher.

Charlotte Ann and her student came into the yard and I was introduced to the boy who had finished his lesson for that day. His eyes sparkled as Charlotte Ann mentioned the piece he should practice before his next lesson.

Never was Charlotte Ann concerned about her clothes, her grades in school, her hair. Her piano playing said it all. She had it made. She was the nearest thing to a celebrity that Edisto Island ever had. All of us schoolgirls were slightly envious, realizing that she had studied under Father Adelard at a Catholic abbey near Moncks Corner. She could be teaching in a school now, or perhaps a college, because she had obtained her degree in music. Like me, probably, she preferred to remain at home for a while. Mrs. Kell came back and led me into a central hall with fourteen- or fifteen-foot ceilings. A spiral stairway rose from the back of the hall to the second floor. Charlotte Ann indicated the music room, which was just off the hall.

The music room wasn't a ballroom, but it was special. The upright piano stood near a window. For a moment I dwelled on the unexpected situation of my having a Baldwin grand and Charlotte Ann using an upright piano. Still, she was a blue blood and the trappings of that class were significant. We sat in straight chairs, facing one another.

She came right to the point. "When do you want to start your lessons?"

"As soon as possible. When can you give me a lesson?"

She went to a desk and opened a book. "You can come on Thursday during the day but if you should choose to come at night,

Tuesday will be better. I charge two dollars and thirty-five cents for a lesson of thirty to forty-five minutes. I will buy your music in Charleston and add the cost to your next lesson's fee."

"May I start next Tuesday night?"

She thought about it for a minute. "I think seven-thirty is good."

While making a note on a page she said, "I'll have a book for you to start on, and we'll go from there." She turned to face me. "I should explain that each year in springtime I have a recital in my home, right here in the music room. When I feel you have progressed enough, you will start practicing to play in the recital. I'll select the piece you will play."

I could hardly believe my ears. I would play her piano, right here in this lovely room, and guests would be sitting in the very chairs I was eyeing. I wondered what Mrs. Kell would serve them. Chocolate milk? I would get a new dress for that occasion. And how! I would go to King Street in Charleston and for the first time in my life I would buy a snazzy dress. Not only would I show off my newly discovered talent for playing the piano, I would exhibit all the grace and poise of a real virtuoso.

Driving home I wanted someone to talk to, to tell about my plans. Daddy was about the only person I knew who was truly interested in my learning to play the piano and he was a person who could listen, but he worked hard and had little time for chats. Mother would listen but she wouldn't understand the depth of my longings, nor would she perceive the hard work involved in learning to play a musical instrument. Little did I know that when I reached home, there in the doorway was the very person for me to ask advice—my little sister.

"Jonny! When did you get home?"

"A while ago. Where've you been?"

As we hugged I whispered into her ear, "You'll never guess."

"Where?"

"Talking with Charlotte Ann Kell. She's going to give me music lessons. Have you seen the piano?"

"Of course."

We went to the living room. I sat on the piano stool and let my fingers run up and down the keys. "Are you going to learn to play it?" I asked my sister.

"Goodness, no," Jonny said. "Music's not my thing." She thought a minute then asked, "Do you have a job yet?"

"No. And as each day passes I know I've got to find my place in the working world."

"Have you thought of what you would like to do?"

"There are several possibilities but nothing that I'm hot on," I explained. My fist just came down on the piano keys and made a blast. "Oops, sorry, but that's about how I feel toward going to work. I'd rather spend my time studying with Charlotte Ann."

Jonny rubbed her lower lip. "You know, there's a very good opening at the courthouse in Walterboro."

"How do you know?"

"Suzy Lyon said her father, the clerk of the Court of Common Pleas, is looking for somebody." Jonny's eyes surveyed me. "You would be perfect for it. *Perfect!* You would work with all the people in the county who go there to do whatever it is they do, pay taxes, sit on a jury, settle estates, you know what they do at the courthouse."

My first thought flew to Mr. Bodicott. I really wanted to get to know him better and give him a tour of Edisto Island and tell him the history of all the old estates. He couldn't appreciate his place in the community until he understood the history and the families. He was an aristocrat, but still, someone needed to clue him in on a few things. Be that as it may, I needed a job. Paying for music lessons was coming up, and I wanted some new clothes. When the time for the recital approached, I would need a dazzling dress. Suddenly I was glad I had scheduled my lessons for Tuesday nights instead of during the day. That would not have worked out. "Let's go to Walterboro and see about that job. Can you go?"

"Get in the car."

As I reached for my purse, Jonny said firmly, "I'm driving!"

Chapter Four

Large letters etched in gold read J. Lester Lyon, Clerk of the Court of Common Pleas. A woman got up from her desk and came to the counter as we walked in. "Good afternoon."

"Hello," I said. "My sister has learned that this office has a job opening. I'm here to talk with someone about it."

"Mr. Lyon is in court right now but he'll be back in about an hour. He is the one you should see."

"Can you tell me anything about the duties that go along with the job?" I asked.

"Mr. Lyon can tell you everything you need to know."

"Thank you," Jonny said. "We'll amble down the street and have a bite and come back." We walked back out on the street. "She wasn't the friendliest person I've ever met," Jonny whispered to me. There were several restaurants on the main street. We entered one that advertised sandwiches. After giving our order, Jonny said, "I stick by my opinion that you will be perfect for the courthouse job. It's government, and you, well, you are sort of a little government within yourself."

"Shut your mouth!" I all but shouted.

"You are. Don't you know it?"

"I am not."

"Well how do you explain your methods of operation? You know, how you keep everything neat, have a place for everything and keep it there, and I've yet to see a form you can't fill out wonderfully. Not to mention your letters. They're masterpieces."

"I don't get you," I uttered.

"You're a little like Mother," Jonny went on.

"Now, I *really* don't get you."

"She does everything she's supposed to do and never asks for help. She cooks, sews, cleans the house. Everything gets done and she has a place for everything. That's so like you."

"She does work hard for us. I don't know what we would do without her, but she never had the opportunity of becoming interested in music or anything related to the arts. It was the way she was raised, having to help with the cooking and washing and helping take care of her brothers. I want to learn to play the piano. I'm not like Mother. I'm more like Daddy's sisters."

"You're going to do everything perfectly. I have no doubt you'll learn to play the piano in record time. Charlotte Ann Kell will never have another student like you."

I paused and for a second almost confided my feelings for Mr. Bodicott to Jonny. I wanted to tell her how I felt, what little I knew of him, ask her what her thoughts on that subject were. I needed to talk to somebody, and Jonny would be perfect, but I just couldn't phrase my thoughts. The words refused to spill out. I was dwelling on them, aching to say them, but something held me back. "No. I don't think I'm brave enough to work at the courthouse."

Jonny took the last bite of her barbeque sandwich and washed it down with a swallow of iced tea. "You're crazy. You'll get the job and everybody in the county will know you and respect you."

"You really believe that?"

"Of course I believe it. It's true. You'll see. Let's go."

This time when we entered the courthouse, the woman behind the counter recognized us and disappeared through a door to the side. She returned with a very tall man with a shock of snowy hair. "This is Mr. Lyon."

"Come with me," he said, leading us through the door into what must have been his office. "Please, sit down." He indicated chairs for Jonny and me. "Miss McLeod, right?" He gave me a smile.

"Yes sir," I responded, maybe a little too loudly. I was feeling quite nervous. I folded my hands together in my lap.

"Where do you live?" he asked.

"Edisto Island."

"Edisto?" He threw back his head and reflected. "Good people out there. They pay their taxes. As honest as the day is long. I know your father. Guess he's busy in the fields right now."

"He is."

"Good, strong Edisto stock." Mr. Lyon shook his head then got down to business. "Let me tell you what this job consists of. I need a deputy clerk of court. There will be a lot of typing. There's one good thing about it: I'm getting one of those electric typewriters. None of my other women want it. They're satisfied with the Royal manual typewriters. I'm buying a Remington electric."

"I've never used an electric typewriter," I said, hoping that Jonny was listening. "But I'd like to try one. I'm sure I could handle it."

"I need somebody who is good with people. There's a place for some help with estates. The folks lose a loved one. They come in here not having the faintest idea what's expected of them. We have to lead them through all the steps of settling up an estate.

"I have two courtroom clerks, but there are days when you would have to be in the courtroom for one reason or another, both civil and criminal court. I always say there's a demeanor in the courtroom and a demeanor for everywhere else. One has to learn from experience how serious courtroom work is. It is no place for frivolity."

"My sister is anything but frivolous," Jonny interjected. "We were talking about that over lunch. She's a rock of Gibraltar. Very serious. Very dependable."

Mr. Lyon looked at Jonny as though he had not realized she was there. "Is that so?" He gazed back at me. "We can pay you fifty dollars a week. When can you start, Miss McLeod?"

"Is Monday all right?"

"Monday is perfect, but that will be a busy day. I must warn you: my court clerks are running in every direction, answering questions, checking the dockets, advising people about lawsuits, and the lawyers just pile into the office on Monday morning, filing complaints, answers, checking real estate titles—a hundred things. Can you be here at 8:30?"

"Yes, sir. Thank you, Mr. Lyon." I decided to go a bit further and shock Jonny. "Uh, Mr. Lyon, I want to thank you for the confidence you have reposed in me. I won't take that lightly. I'll work very hard to make sure you never regret this decision."

Mr. Lyon stood up. "Miss McLeod, I'm sure I'll never regret the decision. We're like one big family, those of us in the courthouse. Glad to have you on board."

"I told you," Jonny said as she started the car. "You do everything exactly right and you don't leave a speck of dust on anything. I'm going to Coker to catch up on some work this summer. When I come home again you'll be running for the office of the clerk of the Court of Common Pleas. Is Mr. Lyon a Democrat or a Republican?"

"Isn't everybody in South Carolina a Democrat?"

Jonny drove on Highway 17, the coastal road, and as we passed the signs designating the islands, Kiawah, Yonges and others, it came to me that I had been fortunate. In the most recent days I had been provided a grand piano and would start taking music lessons next week. On Monday I would become a deputy clerk of the Court of Common Pleas. I wasn't exactly self-supporting but I was self-controlled. Everything else would come in time. Some members of my high school class were already married. Those platinum-haired twins, Callie and Sallie Middleton, had married and now lived in homes on Edisto Island. We'd never been close friends, although I remembered spending the night at the Middleton home once when I was a child. We tried our hand at putting together a jigsaw puzzle on the dining room table. As the twins matured, they told all they saw or heard. It was their worst trait. Everyone on the island knew the talk of Edisto. I guarded against such behavior and as we rode home I silently prayed to God to keep me from being proud, because it did seem that the world was smiling on me. A friendship with Mr. Bodicott seemed the only thing that was slow in developing and my confidence in that area was in a mode of slow growth, as Daddy often referred to his crops in times of drought. But the rains always came and saved the crop.

When Jonny pulled the car in the backyard, Daddy was sitting on the steps, churning a freezer of ice cream. He always made the same flavor, pineapple. I jumped out and began telling him the news. I had gotten a job at the courthouse. I would be working at the county seat! He showed genuine happiness but, as was his nature, he said he wanted to ask me some questions about my duties. Was I sure I was prepared to handle them? He was afraid some of the duties would be over my head. He explained how Edisto Island was located in two different counties, and how some people did business at the Charleston courthouse and others, like us, went to the smaller town of Walterboro.

Mother brought bowls and spoons to the yard. I told her I wanted her to come and visit me in the courthouse and let me show her around. She asked me about transportation, and I thought about Mrs. McKinney, who drove back and forth to her job at a location on the outskirts of Walterboro. I would pay her for transportation. Mother said, "That's my girl. I knew you could do it. I'm proud of you." Daddy smiled and said again that he wanted to hear more about my duties as a deputy clerk of court.

Daddy lifted the dasher out of the churn and placed it on a plate for Mother. She always ate from the dasher, and she ate quickly before the ice cream melted. Eating ice cream from the dasher was somewhat in the manner of the way she chose a piece of fried chicken. She declared that she liked the bony pieces best, but I knew she was saving the white meat for the rest of us. Daddy filled a bowl with a mound of ice cream for Jonny and then one for me. Lastly, he filled one for himself. I always liked to watch him eat ice cream. Instead of jabbing the spoon into the white mound, he carefully started at the bottom and skimmed off a thin layer of the creamy mixture. As he worked his way around the mound of ice cream, the sculpture became firm and clean, like the pictures I had seen of snow-capped mountains in the

Himalayas. If his ice cream were magnified a million times, it would be perfect for the skiers in the Olympics. The *Olympics*.

I had just won the silver and bronze medals, with my job and piano lessons. If Mr. Bodicott allowed me to escort him on a tour of Edisto Island, that would be the gold medal.

Chapter Five

I was wearing my Sunday dress and heels when I decided to walk to the river. Dinner, as we called the midday meal, was over and Jonny was on her way to Hartsville. Except for my thoughts, I was alone when I heard a truck stop at our house. I turned and, believe it or not, it was Mr. Bodicott. He saw me in the distance, waved and walked toward me. He wore casual clothes and I wished I had taken time to change into shorts and a shirt. On the other hand, he had never seen me in a voile dress. It was time he saw me at my best. Everything was good, including the weather. I looked at the sky. Calm and blue. Not a cloud anywhere.

He came closer. "Is the invitation for the tour still open?"

"Of course. Do you want to leave now, or shall we, maybe, just stroll to the river?"

"That sounds good."

The water was a little choppy, a few boats were skimming along in the breeze and, as usual, people fished from the shore. Everything looked perfect. A sailboat passed by in a leisurely glide.

"Like to sail?" he asked.

"We don't have a sailboat," I explained. "Daddy has a pontoon. He takes the family out now and then but uses it mostly for fishing. What about you?"

"I've had my share of boating, all shapes and sizes of vessels." He didn't explain when and where he had been a boatman, but I surmised he had lived near the ocean.

"You like history?" I asked.

"That depends."

I let my eyes drift to the boaters and pretended to be interested in them, but I was aware that he was looking at me. I was thinking, *Depends on what?* No one can escape history. "You're a part of Edisto Island, so I'm assuming you'll enjoy a few tales of the history of the island," I said as I turned around.

"Do the tales concern you?"

The question was a little intrusive, but I took it that he was interested in me.

"Perhaps, if you like."

"How's your progress with the piano?" He stepped toward the marsh area and pulled a reed and put it between his teeth.

"I take my first lesson on Tuesday night. I'll work hard at it. I believe it was Thomas Carlyle who said, 'Blessed is he who has found his work; let him ask no other blessedness.'"

I was careful not to get in oozy mud when I meandered over to the soft porous earth where the reeds were waving toward the sky. I pulled three, held them in my teeth and began to plait them.

"Infused in the audacious interpretation of the responsibility of the unique peculiarities of so celebrated and distinguished a conviction, your future life is surely attributable to the application of this repository." Mr. Bodicott said that. He really did.

For a minute he gazed into my eyes, not in towering confidence of his deed of tongue but awaiting a simple reply, I believed. There was no easy response. Mr. Bodicott had garbled something completely unintelligible to me. How could anyone understand him? How could *I* understand him? Finally I came to the conclusion that I could not understand what he said. Although his phraseology was over my head, I knew what he thought. And I liked it.

Just then I noticed a three-masted clipper ship at full sail. "Look at that," I sang out. "It reminds me of the *Sea Cloud*. She was built for speed. She sailed on this river only once, but she was frequently docked at the Combahee River plantation of her owner, Mrs. E.H. Hutton. Daddy took me there once for a look. I was very little, but I remember that vessel. Fact is I'll never forget it."

"Hutton?"

"Marjorie Merriweather Post was Hutton's second wife. The Huttons had a daughter, Nedenia, but she was known as Dina. Mrs. Hutton was the richest woman in the world and she had her sailing vessel rigged and built for speed. The *Sea Cloud* was a beauty. Mrs. Hutton was an heir to the Post Toasties fortune, and I suppose there was no restriction on the money she spent. Before the Huttons divorced, she built an outstanding home in Palm Beach, Mar-A-Lago. As I said, all of that was long ago, when I was very small, but I remember it as though it were yesterday. For a few brief years Marjorie Merriweather Post Hutton flashed her splendor around Edisto Island. She was the figurehead here. Much the same as the bit of carving with a few streaks of gold leaf at the head of a smooth hull, she led all the rest."

I quickly let up about the Huttons. I could tell that Mr. Bodicott was not at all interested in the very rich. I had to come back down to earth and join him. "The tour is about to begin," I said casually. "Let's not be late."

Chapter Six

$\mathcal{W}$e rode in the cab of Mr. Bodicott's truck and I directed him to the end of Brick House Road. "Stop here. I want you to see the ruins of what once was one of the finest mansions in the country."

When his eyes took in the ruins of so grand a home, he shook his head. "How in the world…?"

"It was very tragic. The Jenkins family, who owns the property today, were inside and escaped without so much as a toothbrush." In order to restore him, I suggested we look closer at the property. On the ocean side of the ruins we gazed across the many miles of marsh. "When the king granted this land in the early 1700s, he included the marshes. That wasn't always done."

He looked up and down the coastline. "You mean that the marshlands belonged to the people who owned this house?"

"Exactly. Not all of the families whose property came from the king's grant were deeded the marshes. And oh, I must tell you about the construction of this house. The blueprints are on file in Washington, D.C."

"Yes, the, uh, blueprints," he said as he took my hand and pulled me up to him. There was a balmy sweet scent to him that was more fragrant as he crushed against me. I was having sensations I'd never before known. I tried to push the thoughts of Daddy away but I almost heard him warning me about certain situations. Mother had never seemed to be able to talk to me about the love of a man, but Daddy had warned me about how men took advantage of some women; especially threatening was the tale of Miss Purseglove on Highway 17. Her family was an old and distinguished one, but she had disgraced them. Daddy had cautioned me that this would never happen in our family. Never in a million years. I pushed away Daddy's voice and all the warnings when I felt Mr. Bodicott's lips upon mine.

"My name is Benjamin," he mumbled.

"Mr. Bodicott is your father," I whispered.

Benjamin relaxed for a moment. Was he thinking of his father, the same sort of interruption as I had felt when I thought of mine? I could feel him slipping away. It had something to do with his father. I had to fix it. "I couldn't care less what your father's name is. You're Benjamin. The name suits you perfectly."

He held me for a moment then kissed my forehead playfully. He was back. I thought he would kiss me on the lips again and turned my face up to his. Instead, he pulled me so close to him that I felt welded to his body. For the first time in my life I could feel my heart beating, but my heart was the least of my thoughts. I had entered a kingdom of peace that had never existed for me. There were no cares, no fears or concerns. There were no music lessons and no job at the courthouse. I knew only that the kingdom was a perfect place and I never wanted to return to the real world again. Finally he let go but I held on. For an instant I divined my right to that kingdom. I was his subject, under his control, and I didn't want to go back to Edisto Island. People in the hospital died, had out-of-body experiences from which they did not desire to be brought back to reality. I had not died, but in the smithy of my marrow I had forged the right to this secret place. Suddenly my consciousness kicked in.

I took hold of his hand. Pulling gently I led him back to the ruins of Brick House. "I thought for a minute you would have to pry each of my fingers loose," I joked. But it was no joke. Something stood silent in my soul.

The labor of ages lay in piles of bricks around what was left of the foundation of the mansion. I reached for one. "Okay, Benjamin. Take this brick. It came from Boston nearly two hundred and fifty years ago."

"Is it mine? To keep?"

"It's yours to have and to hold, but that is the least of the blessings of this house." Benjamin's eyes drifted toward the foundation of the house and piles of loose bricks. "The brick was made for Paul Hamilton, the grandfather of Paul Hamilton III, who was elected governor of South Carolina and appointed secretary of the navy under President James Madison. The brick is Dutch Colonial, from Holland."

"I wonder how thick the walls were. Let's take a look at the foundation." Benjamin strolled in the direction of the ruins.

I caught up with him. "The walls were two feet thick. Facings on corners and under the windowsills were of concrete. The rooms were paneled in cypress—the lumber came from England, but it was seasoned for years before the house was built, about 1703, I think."

Benjamin looked again at the brick he was holding and said he would display it in his store. There were several uses for it he explained.

"About 1798, the property passed into the hands of the Jenkins family," I cautiously continued, being careful not to say the wrong thing. A part of me remained in my kingdom. "They own it today."

"What do they do here?" he asked, spreading an arm toward the ruins.

"They own homes on the island and spend the summers here. They love Brick House so much. When a member of the family dies, that person usually is buried in a cemetery on the island and the family comes here after the funeral. They gather around and talk about their lives in the house before it burned and they receive love and memories and blessings from the ruins. The Jenkinses are all over the island during the summer. They're fun. They love each other to pieces and we all love them."

"Are there other historic places as interesting as this one?"

"Oh my mercy, yes. You'll not believe what I tell you about the Seabrook mansion. But we're first going to Peter's Point. When we go to the church cemetery, I'll show you where the owner of Peter's Point Plantation is buried, but before we go there, we're going to take in a little bit of haunted ground."

As I got into the truck, I wondered if Benjamin was having a good time. I had taken over the day and tried to figure out his conduct. Had I gone beyond the mark on the history of the place? I hadn't been a penetrating wit, but he was anything but indifferent. As I thought about it, he was the essence of courtesy and perked up with each point I made. Considering how little he knew of the place he had adopted for his home, I concluded that he was having the time of his life. "Turn here."

He slowed the truck. "Here? On this dirt road?"

"Right here. If I wanted to show you a place that would knock your socks off from the standpoint of beauty, we'd continue on this road, but I'm going to show you something that might just bowl you over from the standpoint of the ridiculous. Turn left and then pull over under the trees on the right."

"Hmmm. Looks like a cemetery." He turned the truck into a shady spot and turned off the ignition. I slipped off the seat and took a few steps to a dark and musty place. Benjamin looked all around. "Spooky."

"This is where those who were born in slavery, and their descendants, bury their dead." I accidentally stepped on a mound of dirt covering a recent burial site. "Excuse me," I said toward the person lying at rest.

"You think he heard you?"

"I don't know, but the least we can do is be respectful of the people buried here." Among the faded and wilted flowers on the grave was a bottle of medicine and a spoon. I pointed them out.

"What's that doing here?" Benjamin looked at the huge oaks. Spanish moss hanging from the limbs waved in the breeze, not like the wild tail of a dog but gently, like the outgoing tides. "Surely the medicine can be of no use in this place."

"Many of the islanders believe, and they believe it *perfectly*, that if one places on the gravesite the last thing the deceased person used in this world, that item will prevent the spirit of the deceased from returning and taking vengeance on an enemy."

Benjamin walked closer to the bottle and spoon and leaned over them.

"Don't violate the grave," I cautioned. "Should you move the bottle or spoon, you would become one of the enemies of the deceased."

He stepped back. "You believe that?"

"I don't believe it works like the people who placed it there, but I'm a strong supporter of the people who live on this island and adhere to their beliefs. The ideas were planted in their head when they were children."

"Are there other cemeteries with items such as these on the graves?" Benjamin asked.

"Oh, gosh, there are many. Some day I'll take you to a gravesite that is covered in money. Loads of money. Up to your knees."

He looked at me quizzically. "You must be…"

"Plastic bags are filled with quarters. People live nearby. Children shoot balls through hoops just steps away. No one dares to put a finger to the touch test. They shiver at the thought of indemnity of the past and security of the future. But that place is for another day. You probably don't believe half I tell you and a third of what you see, but this is the substance, the core of Edisto. You'll come to understand the people of this island. Let's go."

"You're a good teacher." He gazed toward the sky and laughed a little sarcastically. "The best I've ever had." He shook his head and took my hand as we left. Suddenly he turned and looked back. "I feel strangely at home here. This is where I belong."

That remark was substantial, I thought. He belonged on Edisto, the same as I. I braced myself against showing any emotion.

Making our way on the road through the woods, the Peter's Point mansion suddenly came into view. "That house is where Isaac Jenkins Mikell lived and made his fortune. Some people believe it is the most stunning home on the island, but they haven't seen Mikell's Charleston home. Now there's a mansion if ever there was one."

"He made a fortune here, in these very fields," Benjamin said. "People still grow cotton here, but…"

"But the day and time of the planter aristocracy is gone," I added.

"The boll weevil took care of that," Benjamin added. "We're still fighting it."

I suggested he not drive too close to the house, which was occupied by an active family. "The Charleston house is at 94 Rutledge Avenue, and I can actually take you inside that one. But we've got to hurry on." I indicated a turn in the roadway near the house, and soon we were on our way to the Seabrook Mansion.

The sight of what was known as the Old Seabrook Mansion had a palpable design upon us. Benjamin uttered, "Beauty. Quality."

I added, "Mysteries and stories that touch the soul."

"But it needs some fixing up," Benjamin said.

"That'll come. Wealthy Northern folks are grabbing the old houses and restoring them to their original loveliness."

"If it belonged to me…"

"Are you dreaming?" I almost screamed. "Do you know how much the owners would ask for this historic house?" At once it struck me that perhaps Benjamin *could* own this house. I had no idea how much he was worth, or what he was thinking. Just then a squad of gnats swarmed about us and I suggested we walk around the building. At once it struck me that Benjamin knew nothing of this house and I must give him some perspective on it.

"The Marquis de Lafayette was entertained at this house while touring the South in 1825. Just before the great Frenchman stepped ashore, a carpet was spread a distance of a quarter-mile from the boat landing to the house, so the general would not have to put his foot on common soil." I spread my arms out and added, "The planters from the other big houses on the island attended a reception in Lafayette's honor. Whitmarsh Benjamin Seabrook made the welcoming address right there on that porch. But that's not the best part of the story.

"It was during that reception that the daughter of Lafayette's host was christened. Lafayette requested the honor of naming the little Seabrook daughter Carolina de Lafayette Seabrook. Oh dear," I said as my eyes strayed to my watch, "time is flying and I've simply got to show you the cemetery at the Presbyterian church and the little grocery store near the beach." I was dismayed that time had passed so quickly and said mostly to myself, "We'll surely come back and see all of the old homes."

Benjamin took me by the shoulders and squarely faced me. "Next Sunday?"

"Next Sunday," I answered.

"These houses were built to last for generations—meant to stay in the family. That's what I want for my own house. I'm not a put-on type of person, but I want a house that I, my children and my grandchildren can come home to. A homestead. I trust I'll always have the means, as President Truman said, to make improvements and growth of underdeveloped areas, but for my home, I will spare nothing. I helped my parents and their relatives to bring growth and prosperity to an underdeveloped area, and now I'm giving my attention to my own home."

I have never wanted anything more, I believe, than to ask about his relatives and where that underdeveloped area was, but I had to bide my time. The last thing I desired Benjamin Bodicott to think of me was that I was pushy.

"Edisto Island has a heart, an honor, a quietness…" he began.

"…a solitude that's of itself," I said, finishing his sentence. "It means so much to me, and I can see that you feel the same, but we're still on tour," I said as we made our way to the truck and the next attraction.

"This church is the oldest Presbyterian church in its original location in South Carolina," I explained as we stood in the cemetery behind the church. "The remains of some of the island's most prosperous planters are here. I could show you many but I want you to see the monument at the resting place of Isaac Jenkins Mikell, who owned Peter's Point and the Charleston mansion I told you about." Like a velvet curtain on a stage, my arms unfolded to the view.

Benjamin seemed overcome for a moment. I didn't disturb his solitude. Tears came in little riverlets on his cheeks. Something had entered his soul. If he wanted to share it with me, he would. If not, so be it.

"My mother. She lies in a cemetery on an island." He looked around. "Much like this place." He reached down and lifted a handful of dirt and let it sift through his fingers. "This soil, of which we were made, is a perfect place to be buried."

Every thought Benjamin had shared with me consumed my heart. He loved his mother and that trait in a man was honorable, I believed. He had bequeathed himself to the dirt from which he came. His observation of the plain and simple things was on the mark. Not one to elaborate, he was an honest and good man, the kind any woman would choose for a soul mate. "Where is the island?" I asked. "Where is your mother buried?"

"Off the coast of Georgia."

He seemed to recover his assurance but didn't look at me when he said softly, "Whaley, I want to take you there. To my mother's grave."

That was the first moment that I knew, unequivocally, that Benjamin would ask me to marry him. He was thinking of his mother and of a similar cemetery on an island off the coast of Georgia and I let him explore his thoughts. Under any circumstances the spell would fade all too soon but I had made a momentous discovery of his plans.

I had planned to tell Benjamin the story of the Legare Mausoleum, standing behind the Mikell monument. He couldn't miss seeing the tiny Greek-like temple with Ionic columns that sat there, with no door at the entrance other than the three pieces of marble that lay on the ground at the foot of what once was the door. The story of the young girl who visited the Legare family, died on the island and was laid to rest there was one that many people came to Edisto Island to hear. It was fifteen years after her burial before the true story was known. When a young man in that family died on the battlefield and was sent to Edisto Island for burial, his remains were to be interred in the little mausoleum, alongside the young girl's. The heavy marble door was opened and the skeleton of the young girl fell out into the cemetery. It was then the mourners and family realized the young woman had been prematurely buried, having been in a deep coma and having not died at all. She had endeavored to open the door but the heavy marble would not budge.

Finally, the Legares had their servants wrap heavy chains around the building and locked them with the largest locks of that day and time. Yet, within a week, the chains and locks lay on the ground and the door was standing open. It was the belief of the family that the deceased woman would not allow the door to remain closed, lest someone else be buried alive and not be able to escape. Finally, the door itself fell into pieces on the ground.

Someday I would tell the story to Benjamin, but not now. He was remembering his mother's death on an island, and he would take me there.

❋
Chapter Seven

When you make a right turn at the ocean, you'll see a tiny building on the right, facing the sea. That's the grocery store and it's usually open seven days a week. If it's open, William McClair, a descendant of Edisto slaves, will be sitting on a large barrel, his legs dangling. He tells a story about a voyage to China, a country he refers to as 'Chinee.' You haven't been indoctrinated to Edisto Island until you've heard William's tale."

"I'm ready for it," Benjamin said.

As soon as the truck had made the turn, there was William, sitting on the barrel. "He's waiting for an audience, and that's us," I explained as we left the truck. "William, this is Mr. Benjamin Bodicott."

"I know that man. He own de Feed and Seed."

"He does indeed, and he has come to hear your story."

William scratched his white head, looked at Benjamin and said, "Well, dat's why I'm here. I sit here all day long and tell my story to everbody."

Benjamin leaned against a post and I pulled up a small chair. William looked toward the sea for a moment and said, "Dere's a sea monster out dere. I saw him. And dis is how all of dat came about:

"Well, as I say, we set sail. We sail about two months. De sea been smooth, just like Edisto Islant Crick." (I whispered to Benjamin, "The Edisto River.") "All we boys get along fine. De cap'n was a good man, ain't make we boys work overly hard. We scrub deck now and den, but dat been a small task. We sat down in de shade beneat de mast and main sail and we prank around some and we sing some.

"Things been going too good. Time come when de boys done stop a-prayin. Dey trow down pray when dey pick up cards. Play cassina and seven-up after night, and the Master ain't like dat kind of going on. I hate to give myself praise, but I ain't follow dem bad boys. I keep right on a-praying every night. I thank God for what He done for me and I ask him to keep de cap'n's head leveled on de Char'son side. De ocean flat as a pancake most of de way, but it slant down when you come near South Carolinee. I speck we been 'bout a hundred miles off shore on dat pertikuler day. Lord, it been calm. Never in my born life did I see de ocean so quiet. De sail flutter and we stop moving. I ain't like de way things look, and de cap'n ain't like dem neither. Watch out when the sea get glassy. I be an old sailor, you know, and put my 'pendance 'pon what I done observe while sailing 'round the world.

"Yes, we been stopped dead in we track. Ain't moved an inch for tree whole hours. De sky a-blazing blue, and de sun be hot. I wipe de sweat offer my forehead and wait. Just wait.

"All a sudden I hear a stir in de water off de port side. For a minute I tink it been a porpoise playing 'round, or maybe a shark. But I been wrong. I been dead wrong. A big head stick up. What a head! He patterned after a snake, and he got ugly red eye and scale all over him. No mistake, de thing was a sea serpent as sure as God made de world. De body start for to rise and I notice close. It been big around as a hogshead and covered over with grease. I tell the cap'n, I say, 'Oh, boss man, a sea serpent is off de port side and I tink he's comin' on board.'

"The cap'n make answer: 'Let 'em be, boy. If he come aboard he come aboard. Ain't no help for 'em. It be God's will.'

"All hands gather 'roun den. Dey run to de port side and de ship list over wid de weight. De boys been stand there with their mouths wide open and their eyes fair to pop out dere head. De ting take a grab on a hatch hinge and hoist heself up over de side. We part way and let 'em pass. He crawl slow-like 'cross the deck and leave a greasy track where he been, just like lard lays down.

"I'se a church-going man, but I tremble dat day, I tell you. De cap'n got he hand on de Bible. Dem bad, card-playing boys start for to pray. Too late, boys. God done sent trouble.

"De ting keep right on crawling. Please, Master, he reach the main mast and start for to climb. He go up that mast just like a snake climbing a hickory tree and ain't stop 'till he get to de tip top. All de time he breathe hard like a boa hog and spatter down lard upon top of we heads. Everybody stand stock still. Nobody move an eyelash. We too afraid.

"The serpent been up on top de mast as I done said. He twist 'roun and 'roun de mast so tight I hear de wood crack. Den he cast he eye down and look right in my eye. I never look in sea serpent eye before and I pray to God I never do again. He look like he say, 'Who you think you is anyhow? What I care 'bout mankind? I ain't got you for to study.'

"By and by he start for to crawl down. He come slow, 'fraid he fall, maybe. One de boys take up tackle block and chunk at de serpent. De block hit he square on de head but he ain't seem to mind. Just wink one eye and keep on going.

"De cap'n yell out, 'You done it now. Ain't I tell you for to leave that serpent alone? Bad luck sure to follow us now.'

"That thing on the deck now. Everybody back-to-back and let 'em pass. He take he own good time and grease up the boards just like he done before. He get to de edge of deck and den he crawl over de side, and soon we hear a splash. Dat be de sea serpent goin' down to he home 'neath de ocean.

"Two hour pass and a big wind blow up from de east. De sail belly and we fly along same as a bird. When night come the wind get briefer an' briefer an' de thunder crash and the lightnin' split de sky. We take down every bit of canvas then, all cussing the jib. It been de worstest storm I ever 'sperience in thirty years at sea. He blow and he blow. He blow the lifeboat away and take de cook's cabin off. He strip all de hair off Cap'n's head. He move de hog pen and put 'em in Cap'n's bed. Everyting been mix up, mix up. De wind take all we clothes. When de storm be over we been naked as jaybird.

"But tank de Good Master all on board save. When de wind slow down we knock off work one full hour and fall on we knee and tank God for mercy. We promise not for to play cards again, and we promise perzackly not for to chunk at sea serpent or any of He creatures.

"Nex' mornin' we ketch sight of Saint Philip Church steeple, and we raise a great shout. Home in Char'son once more. Tank Jesus. You done bring us through. All de way from Chinee to Char'son.

"When I get to Edisto Island an' see me wife and eight head of chillun, I start for to think upon de sea and de terrible time I gone through. De sea serpent come back to me in dreams night after night, as I make up my mind to stay right in my home from then on.

"Ain't a living soul can get me back on de ocean again. No sir. No after I look in the sea serpent eye."

Chapter Eight

On Monday morning I walked into the courthouse and marveled again at the grandeur of the large masonry structure. For me to actually work in this place was more than I dared to think. I went into the clerk's office and stood at the counter. Such chaos I had never encountered in my entire life.

"Vestal, do you have the docket?" a man screamed over everybody's head.

"Right here, but I've got to get to the courtroom. Court will convene in a few minutes."

"Is *Fincher v. Burroughs* on the docket?"

The man named Vestal glanced at some papers in his hand. "Yes. Number three."

Mr. Lyon saw me and came from his office. "We've put your desk in the room we call the vault," he explained. "Come with me." We entered a room through a heavy metal round door. The vault was no quieter than the first room. Mr. Lyon pointed out my desk, and I sat down and looked around, trying to get my bearings. Before he had an opportunity to tell me about my job, he was called away by a man I presumed was a lawyer. A lady walked up to me and asked if I would make a copy of her grandmother's will. I didn't know what to say. I looked around and saw a man in a sort of cage. He was accepting payments for something or other. "How can this lady get a copy of her grandmother's will?" I asked.

The man, who I assumed was the bookkeeper, came out and talked with the lady. I went back to my desk. A woman in a green suit came over to me. "I'm Tommie. I know you are new, but can you proofread this with me?" She handed me a two-page document and began to read from an identical paper in her hand: "*The State of South Carolina v. Robert Lohand. The State of South Carolina v. James Calvert. The State of South Carolina v. Mayce Arndt.*" And on and on she read. I found no typos.

"Can you tell me what we just read?" I asked.

"That's the docket for Criminal Court. I'm the court clerk in that courtroom. Vestal works in the courtroom where civil cases are tried." She put the pages into a briefcase and flew out of the office.

Fifteen minutes later a lady ran into the vault and said to everybody, "Oh, happy day. I'm a divorcée." She waved to the air and breezed out as quickly as she had come in. I looked around and some of the other workers were spreading their hands in disbelief. A group strolled in and asked me where the hearing regarding the adoption was being held. The answer was called out over my head, "In Mr. Lyon's office."

In an isolated moment, I let my eyes check out the vault door. My desk was nearest to the entrance to the vault and everybody who entered passed my station. The door was of metal, and at least fifteen inches thick. It was the only entrance or exit to that room. The combination lock was impressive. Obviously the door was locked at the end of the day and all documents in the file folders on the shelves that lined the walls of the large room were safe from vandalism.

Men who I assumed were lawyers entered and left constantly. I looked forward to the time when I knew them better, and felt something of the little lives they left in the safety of the vault. One of the lawyers noticed me watching him as he gathered his notes. "Good morning," he said. He put his papers in his briefcase and walked to my desk. "I'm Guy Henkel."

"Whaley McLeod. This is my first day on the job, but of course you know that already."

"Everybody has a first day on the job and you seem to be doing quite well. If they don't treat you right in here, come across the street and join us. Our firm is always in need of a good secretary."

Guy Henkel left quickly, but others accumulated around the big books that had the information one needed for use in constructing a chain of title. A man who seemed too young to have graduated from law school opened a leather case and removed a typewriter. He searched the big books and typed his notes. No legal pads for him.

Just then Mr. Lyon rushed to me. "Whaley, do you mind taking these papers to Vestal? He needs them now." I got up quickly. It wasn't lost on me that he called me by my first name and I was glad.

I don't know why I ran instead of walking, but I did. When I came to the steps I took them two at a time. I was telling myself that Mr. Lyon had said Vestal needed the papers now, and if anyone judged my worth as a person by dignity, they just didn't know me. For some time now I had worked at composing a sort of credo, and the best I had come up with so far was that I would do nothing merely because it contributed to availability, comfort or prestige. I hoped anything I did would matter in one important way or another.

The bailiff opened the heavy oak door. I stepped inside and saw several men huddled at the judge's bench. Vestal was watching for me. He met me in the aisle and took the papers.

I hurried out. For a brief moment I had been in a sort of sanctified place: dark paneling, men in gray suits, everyone appearing to be in a serious frame of mind, with muted voices and furrowed brows. I was glad to get back to my desk in the clerk's office.

The rest of my day was used in typing a very long will. The electric typewriter wasn't difficult to learn and was working faster and more accurately than a manual one. I learned a lot about one of Colleton County's most renowned families. As I placed the papers neatly in a file folder, I was thinking, "So this is what wealthy people do with their money."

I strolled around the room and chatted for a moment with each employee. Mr. Morgan sat at a huge wooden desk. Lawyers filed papers such as complaints, answers and other documents relating to jurisprudence at this desk. "This must be the place where a lawsuit starts," I said.

"Exactly. It begins right here," he said. He was pleasant enough but not chatty. Someone mentioned he had once owned a baseball team and was interested in athletics, but you couldn't tell it to look at him.

The man in the cage-like enclosure was Mr. Smith, and he was indeed the bookkeeper. Mrs. Moffitt sat toward the back of the room. She typed on very large pages that were kept in the huge books on the counters. Her typewriter was especially made for such large pages, I believed.

The last of the employees in the room was Mrs. Lingle. She worked solely with people who were settling the estates of relatives who had passed away. She appeared to have a little corporation under her control. She opened one large book after another and explained facts to people. She helped them fill out forms, gave instructions as to what was needed and explained in the kindest possible way that she was available should they need her help with any of the steps toward the final document. She appeared to be almost too friendly with the administrators and executors of the estates, but she was only mildly friendly to me.

When I stood on the street corner that day, waiting for my ride with Mrs. McKinney back to Edisto Island, I felt like a different person from the one who had arrived there that morning. It was clear that I worked in an exciting, rather frantic place. I had taken a big step and was looking forward to tomorrow.

Chapter Nine

I walked into the clerk's office the next morning feeling astir and with the world before me. If there had been a song in my heart, it would be entitled "A Man Waits for Me." Benjamin was at the helm of my ship, steering calmly and self-contained, taking me ever closer to the goals that mattered. I thought about my goals a lot, which included getting what I wanted from life and enjoying doing it. Considering present circumstances, the aims were all but ordained. I had found the perfect man. Sometimes he spouted off in polysyllables that were meaningless to his audience, but he used the best words and they made sense to him. I trusted that, in accord with the Constitution, we would form a perfect union. As I thought about it, I had done enough to fill an ordinary life but I could feel the stirrings of a new life, all before me. One of the first steps of preparation for my new life was my first music lesson, which was just hours away. I was filled with anticipation over the lesson but my musings were interrupted when I was called to Mr. Lyon's office.

My boss explained that the bookkeeper had asked for me to be assigned to work for him. I would be known as Mr. Smith's secretary. He collected fees—all sorts of fees—and he would take care of all of that. He needed a secretary to record the checks as they came in and went out and type the amounts into a monthly statement of record. According to the accountability of the clerk's office, the statements I prepared would be important but not self-consuming. Besides Mr. Smith needing a secretary, Judge Parker had asked if one of the ladies in the clerk's office could type his letters. Judges were moved from district to district and had no secretary in any courthouse. I had seen Judge Parker and liked him. From my quick appraisal he seemed to be an honest and fair judge and a pleasant man. I jumped at the chance to work for Judge Parker. *Judge Parker's secretary* sounded rather sophisticated. After I sat down at my desk Mr. Smith called out, "Whaley, bring your notebook." That brought me down to earth.

The fees that had been collected that month were read to me and I jotted them down on my shorthand pad. I was surprised to learn that some alimony payments came and went over Mr. Smith's desk. I was amazed that such a large amount of money was accounted for. After I finished typing the money trail that made its way to and from Mr. Smith's office, I was asked to go to the Criminal Court and deliver a file folder to Tommie. My duties were taking on the mode of commonplace tasks but they had a sort of measured cadence that pleased me.

After lunch Mr. Lyon asked me to accompany a group of people to the bank. Their grandmother's lock box was to be opened by the family and I was to remove the contents of the bank box, list every item on a yellow pad and come back to the office and type the list. I didn't know the reason for the request, but I was asked to send a copy of the inventory to the secretary of State. I was to bring back any copies of a last will and testament that were found in the box. A bank employee would oversee the proceeding.

I joined the family and we walked down the street to the bank. A granddaughter of the deceased person mentioned that it was a hot day and she believed when the weather was very hot, any little ailment a person suffered was more intense. I agreed with her even though I didn't know whether she was right or wrong.

Very little activity was taking place in the bank when we entered. I was thinking that my job was anything but humdrum as I followed the bank employee who carried the box from the bank vault to a small room. The attendant opened the box and indicated it to me. I placed my yellow pad on the table and lifted out several papers. There were some shares of common stock and preferred stock, a few U.S. savings bonds and a will. Then, pay dirt: there before me were seven envelopes filled with hundred dollar bills. I carefully counted the money and made a note of it. Then, on a whim that I was doing the right thing, I asked the bank employee to recount the money. He did and his total agreed with mine. I asked the bank man to add his initials to mine, which I scribbled above the amount of money I had written on the pad. By the time I returned to the clerk's office and typed the inventory of the contents of the lock box, I was exhausted. I made several copies of the inventory and mailed one to the secretary of State. It occurred to me that I should keep the original inventory, made on the yellow pad. After labeling a folder "Inventories of Lock Box Contents," I placed the original inside and slipped it in my bottom desk drawer. The day had tested my durability and my first music lesson was yet before me.

Chapter Ten

*I*t was nine o'clock or thereabouts when I was driving home from the Kell dairy farm. My first music lesson had come and gone and I had come to the conclusion that it requires a courageous person to take on music lessons at my age. I figured that a fourth-grade student would be the perfect person to take it on. All the scales, the whole notes, the half notes, the treble and bass, the crescendo and decrescendo and a whole lot more was as much as a young person, with life stretched out before him or her, could absorb a little at a time. Perhaps people beyond that station in life should be satisfied to appropriate themselves as a silent spectator of some activities, and to take an interest and curiosity in the mighty scheme but not feel the slightest inclination to butt in. And then I pictured the Baldwin grand and I thought of Daddy and the superabundance of joy he was getting just watching the instrument sit there. Fate seemed to be discharging its influence over me. I had no concept of its vision for my life but there was no question something *was* working for me. That unsought influence must have been at work at that moment, because, almost without realizing it, I turned the car into the parking area of the Feed and Seed. Oh my mercy, I couldn't believe I had done that, but I did and there sat Benjamin in a rocker on the porch. He had seen me and waved, and it was too late to turn around. I turned off the ignition and joined Benjamin.

"I'm closed for business," he joked.

"I'm not here on business."

I felt that I was on a stage, performing in a tragic play. I was a heroine who desired from the depths of her heart to face her friend, tell him her hopes and fears, pour out her longings. I wanted Benjamin to climb out of the limitations of his own character and allow me to tap the subtlety of his intellect. I wanted him to review the book of my life, a chapter at a time—the job, the music lesson, the piano—just string it out in the routine of my existence. Hearing the voices of the thoughts somewhere far away in my mind, I wondered if there was any logic in my insanity. Was my mind overtaxed or was I just a little tired? I stood awkwardly. Benjamin was looking up expectantly at me to see what had brought me unannounced.

"My first music lesson is behind me."

"Tell me about it."

"You don't really want to know. It wasn't easy."

"I want to know everything about you, Whaley," he said.

He truly was interested, I thought. *He had escaped some of his limitations and was interested in me. He had opened a door that I thought was closed. In a few words, he was saying, "Whaley, come on in."*

"I came here to invite you to accompany me to Charlotte Ann's concert at the Church of the Tides. She's going to play the new pipe organ for the first time. I can hardly wait."

"I'd like to go with you. When is the concert?"

I couldn't remember the exact day but I didn't want Benjamin to know it had skipped my mind. "It's on a Saturday night and when I get confirmation of the date I'll let you know. Eight p.m." I hoped he would take my explanation for the visit as the truth, although I knew I was lying when I said I had come to issue the invitation. I hadn't actually thought about it until a second or two before the words rolled out. I was uncomfortable. Perhaps this wasn't a good time to call on Benjamin.

"Now tell me how the lesson went."

"Oh, so-so. I'm a little daunted, but I survived."

"Come with me." He got up.

I tried to casually wipe my clammy hands on my dress and followed him through the store, down a hallway and into a rather lovely sitting area. "Do you live here?"

"For now. It's not my forever home."

I wondered what he meant, but I let that pass without responding and he opened a door that unveiled an immortal place. I stepped across the threshold into a sublime, silent, golden existence and I couldn't utter a word. "Welcome to my gardens. There are two, one for food and one for beauty."

All of it was beyond my conception. My voice finally found me. "Beyond all space and time, in Heaven, can anything be more beautiful than this place?"

"There are many that are more beautiful than this," he answered.

I meandered over to huge, curly, kinky heads of lettuce and green bell peppers as large as some beach balls, their forest green leaves falling thick and cool over them. Jasmine vines ran on trellises. Feathery dill bordered fairytale walkways glistening in the tender eventide. Yellow crookneck squash peeked at me from the comfort of its own huge protective leaves. Onions had green shoots. Cucumber vines were nearly a foot high.

In a daze of such beauty I wandered to a hedgerow of hydrangeas. Balls of pink and blue hung their heads amidst the wavy leaves. Tomatoes bulged full, some climbing, many staked with rods three feet in height. Muscadine vines climbed on trees and trellises. I entered a cloister of apple, cherry and fig trees—a place where one could lose oneself in thought. How could anyone say this was not a forever home? Surely he would miss the sanctity of this quiet place should he ever leave it.

Benjamin guided me through a haze of grape-like bunches of flowers to a wooden bench. We sat down. He again asked me about the music lesson.

"It was difficult from the minute I walked into the music room. I expected to play so easily, like Charlotte Ann. But I have to get through this. It's something I cannot fail, because of my father. He bought me the Baldwin grand and now the rest is up to me. It won't be easy. Charlotte Ann provided me a yellow book. I believe Shirmer is the name of the publisher. I'll be using that book for a while. Likely a *very long* while. She started me on the first piece in the book but most of this lesson was about middle C and the scales, which I must practice many times each day. She played a simple piece, counting the time, one-and-two-and, three-and-four-and. Over and over she said that. I'm glad Daddy bought the metronome to help me with timing. Right now I'm overwhelmed. I'll learn to play the piano but I never knew it would be this complicated. And you, while I'm slaving away at the notes, you will be here in this lovely garden, beautiful beyond words. This place has to be yours forever."

"Do you know anything about the Old Brothers Place?" Benjamin asked, changing the subject.

"Oh, do I! We played there as youngsters. Most of the land is in fields, and I went bird hunting there with Daddy. He liked to hunt quail there because there were so many coveys of them in the fields. And right smack in the middle there are several acres that have the most gorgeous oaks."

Benjamin interrupted my reverie. "I've made a bid on that place." He said it as though it were the most natural thing in the world.

"You've made a bid on the Old Brothers Place?"

"Yes. All of it. Three hundred and ninety acres."

"Why do you want it?"

"The Feed and Seed is my business. I want a home. A substantial home. A house I can be proud of."

Benjamin's demeanor seemed to be stirred by the plans for a dwelling, very likely a lovely one. His mind was reeling and I braced myself for one of his garbled speeches that I couldn't fully understand but would appreciate. If it came, I would view it with no misgivings, undaunted and inflexible. The speech didn't come as quickly as I expected.

"Brick, stone and marble. A house of power. That's what I'll have."

Is his reach exceeding his grasp? I wondered. His wealth must be boundless, I thought, but where did he get his riches? I couldn't just ask him his worth. Certainly I knew better than that. I was stupefied but was quickly resurrected by his outpouring of words.

"Phenomenal continuity, philanthropy for each and for all, indisputable. Innovative. Quintessentially coastal. Cornerstone of serenity. Ambience. Craftsmanship. Nature multitasking civilization. All-powerful. Irresolute affairs. Inexorable."

I'm sure he said more, but it was only these beautiful words that caught my attention. Benjamin's passion shocked me. He believed the reaching of his goal was not unconquerable. If I had been rocked by his speech, every pillar of my being was twitched by his next sentence. His eyes flashed peacock blue and his hair ricocheted on his forehead as he moved his head. "I want you to live there with me. Will you do that, Whaley?"

Benjamin Bodicott had just asked me to marry him. I had thought of proposals many times and wondered what mine would be like. I never considered just what the proper lady's answer would be. I didn't want to gush and act so eager he would fear he had made a mistake, and I didn't want to turn him down either. He was a good man. With him there was never a truce between virtue and vice. I said nothing as I thought about the situation. Benjamin was going to elevate his position by the conscious endeavor of building a beautiful home—an estate, really. If I had been interested in spending my life with any other man, there was none that could provide for me in the manner of Benjamin. I took his hand and held it to my cheek. All I could think of as a response was, "Yes."

Chapter Eleven

Two weeks later, on a Saturday evening, Benjamin and I were nearly the last of the people to enter the Church of the Tides. Each of us took a program that was handed to us. We held hands as we slid into a pew near the back. He glanced at me. I glanced at him. We had a secret. We were going to be married. Not right away—I wanted to get a solid start on my music lessons and show Daddy my appreciation for the piano. Daddy had casually mentioned he would like for me to learn to play "Maria Elena," a piece an old girlfriend had played many times for him. What a surprise to learn that Daddy had had a girlfriend other than Mother. It didn't seem possible, but I intended to buy the piece soon and ask Charlotte Ann to play it for me. Benjamin wanted to finish construction of his house before we married. The closing on the Old Brothers Place would take place at the end of the month but the building of the house would take much longer. We agreed to keep our secret, at least for a while.

"Excuse me, excuse me," someone said as she pushed and shuffled her way to sit beside me. It was Mother. And Daddy was behind her. Benjamin and I hastily shifted and released each other's hands. Mother huddled close to me. Her body felt cold. Daddy looked toward the darkened congregation settled on the pews in front of us. He blinked his eyes several times. I pretended I was not surprised to see them.

Daddy leaned over and shook Benjamin's hand. "So the Feed and Seed is on the town tonight."

Benjamin nodded. "Yes, sir." Just then the lights dimmed and a spotlight shined on the lovely pipe organ. No one spoke. I don't believe anyone breathed. Charlotte Ann quietly but quickly walked to the organ and slid across the bench, not glancing toward the congregation. She wore a long black robe. Her only ornament was a choker of tiny sparkling beads at her neck. The small beads formed a wee line that glinted between her blonde hair and the white collar on the black robe. She moved her head slightly as her fingers and feet made their way across the keyboards. Her hair glistened in the light. I was unexpectedly filled with awe. *Am I going to cry?* I wondered. *Or laugh?* In my dazed and wonder-struck condition I knew that I would never forget the dazzle of that evening. My mind abandoned every person and everything in the church except Charlotte Ann and the new pipe organ. I was on familiar turf but the music elevated me to Carnegie Hall. This wasn't "Row, Row, Row Your Boat." I didn't know what it would take to bring me back to reality, but for that moment reality didn't threaten me. I was one, united, complete and fulfilled with the music. I dedicated myself not to forsake my music lessons with Charlotte Ann. I hadn't learned the tip of the iceberg about playing the piano and seven-eighths of all icebergs were under water, yet to be encountered. How small I felt as I watched the virtuosity of Charlotte Ann. I thought of what the novelist Thomas Wolfe had written about fifteen years earlier in his book *You Can't Go Home Again*: If a man has a talent and cannot use it, he has failed. If he has a talent and uses only half of it, he has partly failed. If he has a talent and learns somehow to use the whole of it, he has gloriously succeeded, and won a satisfaction and a triumph few men ever know. Charlotte Ann knew how to use the whole of her talent.

She had started her concert by playing George Frederick Handel's "Water Music." I was familiar with that work of the German composer. No one was talking, and that was a sign of hearing good music, I believed. I was rapt for the rest of the program. Following "Water Music," Charlotte Ann played excerpts from Johann Sebastian Bach's Fugue in D Minor, the "Wedding March" by Felix Mendelssohn, Schubert's "Ave Maria," Beethoven's "Moonlight Sonata" and Handel's Organ Concerto, opus 4, no. 5. The concert ended with a rendition of Handel's "Hallelujah Chorus" from the *Messiah*.

"Ave Maria" surely would be played at my wedding. I didn't want to dwell or think on that subject because I hadn't told Mother and Daddy about it, but suddenly I had the urge to be married at home, with Charlotte Ann playing the Baldwin grand. As I thought about it, I figured we could invite about sixty people. Mother would bring out the good china and I would see that a wedding cake sat on the dining room table. Daddy would be so happy. He liked Benjamin and it was no secret that Benjamin would provide for me. I planned to tell him a few things about Benjamin, and one of them was that I would never suffer from human wants. I could go so far as to tell Daddy that Benjamin would spoil me, perhaps even more than he had done, but then again, maybe I wouldn't go into that.

I could hardly wait to tell Benjamin that I wanted to be married at home and at the appropriate time I would ask Charlotte Ann to play the piano. When the time came to confide in him, I would snuggle close and almost whisper my plans concerning the wedding. I didn't want him to think I was in a hurry for the marriage to take place. I would emphasize that I wasn't trying to rush things up, because in consideration of my beloved's desires we would wait until his house was completed, and I did intend to work hard on my music in the meantime.

When we entered the Fellowship Hall for the reception, Charlotte Ann was surrounded by well-wishers. We waited our turn. I introduced Benjamin and hugged her. I was so overwhelmed with emotion I couldn't help whispering in her ear, "You played several pieces that I want you to play at my wedding."

Charlotte Ann held me back and looked at me. "Is there something you haven't told me?"

"Oh, no," I said, though I'm sure I blushed.

Benjamin and I walked Mother and Daddy to their car. I told them I would see them a little later. We took our time making our way back to Benjamin's truck and heading home. After he pulled into the parking area near our house we sat for a while in the truck. We talked about the wedding, and I told him my plans. He agreed with everything. He especially wanted Charlotte Ann to play the Baldwin grand on that occasion. Benjamin walked me to the door and we kissed goodnight.

Mother and Daddy were still up, sitting in a small area in the back of the house. We called that place the "Little Room." "Whaley," Daddy began, "I just want you to know that I think Benjamin is as near an honest and perfect man as you'll find."

Mother was crocheting an afghan. She didn't look up. "You look well together. You're both tall and hold your heads up straight."

At that moment someone opened the front door and yelled, "Guess who's here!"

It was Jonny. I ran to her and had to bite my tongue from telling her about my plans to marry Benjamin. She would be thrilled but she was one who would have to crow about it to everybody she saw.

I had been tired and ready for bed after a long day, but now the excitement of seeing Jonny made me feel wide awake. "How long will you be home this time?" I wanted to know.

"'Bout a week, give or take a little."

I don't know why I had such a feeling of blessedness for her company but my thoughts of her strung together like the paper dolls we once played with. She knew who I was, what I was about, and when I needed her she was more than just family.

Chapter Twelve

$\mathscr{M}$r. Smith called me to bring my notebook almost as soon as I arrived at work on Tuesday morning. He was dictating and I was recording every word when Mr. Lyon appeared at Mr. Smith's cage. His voice was subdued and the usual sparkle in his eyes was missing.

"Whaley, can I see you in my office please?"

"Yes, sir." I followed him back to his office. He closed the door and asked me to sit down. He sat down at his desk and I believed he was not preoccupied with anything except what he was about to say.

"Whaley, your sister called. They're taking your father to Roper Hospital in Charleston. She'd like for you to meet them there."

Thunderstruck, I sat as if paralyzed.

"I haven't said anything to the others. I'll drive you to Charleston and I'll stay with you until we know what the situation is. I'll get my car and meet you at the front door."

In the car, I asked if Jonny said anything about what had happened to Daddy. "No. She said only that she believed you should come to the hospital. I told her I would drive you there at once. She's expecting you."

Not only were Mr. Lyon's words clear in my ear but also the words he didn't say. *Daddy is being rushed to the hospital. They want me there. Was it an accident?* I wondered. He often drove the tractor in places that appeared dangerous. Some of the ditches were deep and the sand was loose enough to cave in. He fished in the deep waters of the Edisto River when the tides were coming in and flowing back to the sea. Had he drowned? Was he alive? I placed my hands over my face and pictured him, thinking deeply, *Daddy come to me. Are you all right?*

After the hour's drive to Charleston, which we spent mainly in silence, as I was too preoccupied with worry to make conversation, Mr. Lyon pulled into a parking place at the hospital and we left the car quickly. He held my elbow as we made our way inside. He said something to a nurse and she pointed us to a hallway. I could see Mother. She was sobbing. Jonny saw us and ran to me.

"What happened?"

"Daddy had been on the tractor—"

"Oh, my, no."

"It had nothing to do with the tractor," Jonny rushed on. "He drove back to the house and noticed that the yard needed mowing. He pushed the lawn mower for a couple of hours and came to the front door. Mother saw him. He didn't fall until he was in the living room."

"Was he conscious?"

"Yes. He told Mother that he was very tired. He thought he could make it to the house but got no farther than the living room. She called Dr. Taylor. He examined him on the floor and called for an ambulance."

"Was it a heart attack?"

"I don't think so," Jonny said. "Dr. Taylor said there is something about the stomach that has to be dealt with."

"What in the world…"

Jonny hugged me. "I know. Isn't it awful? I never thought anything would happen to Daddy."

I pulled away. "Nothing has happened to Daddy. He's so strong. This is just a minor thing."

Mr. Lyon asked Jonny if there was anything else he could do and she said no. He left the hospital and we walked to Mother. I didn't question her. Dr. Bost came out to talk with us.

I jumped up off the stiff couch. "How's Daddy?" I asked.

"The X-rays show a stomach tumor. We're going to have to schedule him for surgery."

"Oh, no. Is it, you know, serious?" Jonny asked.

"We won't know much about the tumor until we go inside."

"When will you operate?" my mother asked him weakly.

"We should be able to get him in tomorrow morning. There's really nothing more you can do for him tonight. Get some rest. There's a waiting room on the second floor for families of patients undergoing surgery. As soon as I know anything I'll meet you there and we'll talk about it."

Dr. Bost left in a flash. He didn't give us a second to think about what was happening. We found the waiting room and Mother sat between Jonny and me. "I can't help but believe he'll be all right," Jonny said. "He's a tough one. If anyone can come through this he can."

Another family was waiting to hear the news of their patient. We nodded our heads to them and they did the same. Worried expressions covered their faces, the same as ours. The phone in the hallway rang. I answered it. Someone asked for the family of Arthur Stone. I asked the other family if they were there for Arthur Stone, and they indicated they were not. I explained that to the caller. After I put the phone in the cradle, the family of Arthur Stone came in. They looked devastated. I told them someone had called. It was clear we were not the only ones in distress, but that made the suffering no easier to bear.

A nurse came in and told us Daddy was resting now, and would go into surgery first thing tomorrow morning. It would be a while before we would hear anything. She suggested we go to the basement of the building and eat some supper. It was a good suggestion.

Jonny lined up three trays and helped Mother select what she thought she could eat. None of us was hungry. I watched as we pretended to want this or that, but I knew that none of us was sure the food would stay down if it was eaten. We got through the process and went back to the waiting room. We decided not to try to drive back home to Edisto that night, but to pass the night in the hospital so that we would be there first thing the next morning when Daddy got out of surgery. A woman was sitting at a desk. I asked if she had any spare magazines or a newspaper we could read to pass the time.

The night passed fitfully and seemed to last forever. When the light outside began filtering through the windows we blinked at each other and made our way to the coffee pot kept for families like ours. Finally, around eight o'clock, Dr. Bost walked in and motioned for us to come into the hall. He had on his scrubs but removed his cap and talked almost in a whisper.

"The stomach tumor was large," he said. "We removed almost all of the stomach. He'll be in the hospital for a couple of weeks or more. Just let him rest today. He'll be better tomorrow."

"Did you get all of it?" I asked, specifically avoiding the word cancer. That terrible, terrifying word swept people away and swallowed up entire families, and I had no desire for it to be incorporated into my vocabulary.

"We think we did," Dr. Bost answered, mercifully ignoring the dreaded word but alluding to it. "We did not explore the area of the esophagus." He shook our hands and said he would be in and out of the room the rest of the day. He suggested we go see Daddy and then go home and get some rest.

On the way home, I asked Jonny to let me out at the Feed and Seed. I told her that Benjamin would drive me home later in the day. Jonny knew that Benjamin and I were close and it was difficult not letting her in on our engagement. I just couldn't talk of that. Not now.

When I saw Benjamin I dissolved in his arms, telling him in whimpers all that had happened and going into speeches about our affection for Daddy. Benjamin finally calmed me.

"Dry your tears. You need to get some rest. We can go back up to the hospital later today. Why don't you go home and stretch out for a while. I'll pick you up after lunch."

I did as he suggested and he was right. I felt much refreshed after a nice nap and a soothing shower. When Benjamin pulled up in the driveway after lunch, I kissed him lightly on the cheek and slid into the truck. When we got to the hospital, I led the way to Daddy's room. Nurses were around the bed but they allowed us in. Daddy had not regained consciousness. I noticed his long-fingered hands. Wonderful hands. Suddenly a lifetime of those hands filled me with sorrow. They were the hands that had thrown me into the air and caught me as I came down, the hands that had taught me to swim, had saved me from danger, patted my head after many falls. The hands gently moved to the very site of the surgery. He rested them over his stomach, or what was left of it.

"He's in pain. I know it," I said. "He's holding his stomach."

"Your father is in no pain," a nurse said calmly. "We will not allow him to feel pain for at least three days."

Just at that moment I saw one eye open slightly.

"He's awake," I said. I held my head over his face and asked, "Daddy? Can you hear me?" Benjamin was right behind me, his hands on my shoulders. "Daddy, can you hear me?"

Daddy nodded slightly. "Whaley, listen…listen…to me." Daddy's voice was weak. He might utter a word or two, I thought, or he might fall asleep. I put my face to his.

"I'm listening, Daddy."

"Whaley?" He took a long breath. "I, uh, don't know how I'm going to handle this."

"What is it, Daddy? I'll handle it for you. I'll do anything for you, Daddy."

He frowned, irked with the interruption.

"I don't know yet how to handle it, but the piano is yours."

"The piano? Don't worry about the piano now, Daddy. It's not—"

"It's yours. I'm going to see to it."

Suddenly Daddy phased out and was asleep again. "Let's go," Benjamin said. "We don't want him to overdo it."

We walked out of the room and left for home.

We spent most of the ride home in our own silences, but around the turn onto Highway 174 Benjamin finally said, "Your father wants you to know the piano is yours. That's important to him."

"What a thing to think about at a time like this," I reiterated. "I don't want the piano," I croaked. "I want Daddy. The Baldwin grand is wonderful but under present circumstances, it is nothing. *Nothing.*"

"Whaley, there will be better times. I promise you. I've been through this. I know."

For the first time my thoughts went to Benjamin's parents. I didn't know anything about them except that his mother had been buried on an island. I had been remiss in not showing more concern for them, but right now I had my own things to think about.

It was after dusk when we pulled into the driveway of my house. Benjamin walked me to the door. Jonny was there. "Take care of her," Benjamin said.

"I promise," Jonny said.

84

Chapter Thirteen

*N*ot long after Daddy arrived home from the hospital, I realized that life as I had known it would never be the same again. Mother, Jonny and I watched his recuperation in silent horror—not unlike the way we watched storm clouds gather when a hurricane was predicted for the coastal area of South Carolina. First there were the bands of rain and wind, and then the real clouds spread upon the horizon.

The first phase of the convalescence effort involved dealing with medication to relieve the pain. Daddy seemed to be in fairly good spirits after all he'd been through. One of us was with him almost all day until we tucked him in at night. None of us had been through enough hardship to have a perspective on the current situation, but as I watched the islanders bringing food to the door, mowing the lawn and taking care of a hundred other chores, it made a huge and I believe lasting difference in my belief of the importance of the generosity of humankind in times of need. Daddy had contributed to them and their causes all of his life, but I never expected such an outpouring of love and care.

Mr. Lyon was bighearted and gave me time away from work, but after three weeks I went back to the job, catching my ride early in the morning and getting home about six in the evening. Jonny had discontinued her studies for the time being, saying she could not possibly be away from us during these days of longing and prevailing. I took a music lesson every other week instead of each week. Music wasn't a very high priority with me during that sad time, but I knew that would change sometime in the future. Daddy's words, "The piano is yours," played in my head day and night.

As time went on, Daddy's appetite began to fail him. Mother made his favorite soup, something he always enjoyed, but after a spoonful or two, he pushed back the bowl. One morning he said he had a toothache. When I got home from work that day, his jaw was swollen.

The following morning, Mother and Jonny and I tucked Daddy into the car for a visit to the dentist. Jonny drove him there and I caught my ride and went to work as usual. During the afternoon Jonny called me and said that Daddy had seventeen infected teeth and he was in the chair awaiting the removal of them. I asked if Daddy would be under anesthesia, and Jonny assured me he would be. When I got home that evening, Daddy was propped up in his bed, his mouth wide open and stuffed with bloody gauze. His eyes were sunken in and bugged out at the same time. An expression of horror spread across his face. No sound came from him. He was the most pitiful human being on whom my eyes ever had glanced.

About eight o'clock Benjamin drove into the yard. I went out to meet him and tell him what to expect when he saw Daddy. I warned him it was a sight he would never forget. Daddy was an old man in a dream, not the real life person we knew and loved.

We walked into the room, and when Daddy saw Benjamin he uttered a syllable or two. Mother and I tried to calm him, but his eyes were wild and he barked noises that were unintelligible. "Next Fri…day," he gasped. A crooked finger pointed to me. "Her birthday," Daddy spat, with bloody saliva going in all directions.

Benjamin looked at me. "Next Friday is your birthday?"

"Oh who cares?" I said. "That's the last thing I want to think about."

Benjamin didn't stay for a long visit. After he left, Mother, Jonny and I went into the Little Room and talked about Daddy remembering that next Friday was my birthday. His body was weak and his mortality weighed heavily upon him like it was boding some strange eruption. It was the most amazing thing that he would remember my birthday.

Chapter Fourteen

*I*t was the day Mrs. McKinney and I were an hour and a half late getting home. I knew something was wrong. It was mid-August and the summer humidity held fast. Mother was sitting on the porch, a sweater pulled over her shoulders. She looked half-dead. Callie and Sallie Middleton, in matching plaid skirts and crisp white tops, sat with her. *What are they doing here?* I hadn't seen them in ages and that had been okay by me.

As I ran to Mother, Callie said, "Your dad has taken a turn for the worse."

I flew into the house. Jonny was with Daddy, who looked pale and drawn. Suddenly a scream as shrill as that of a stallion being pushed into his slot at a Jockey Club race emerged from Daddy's throat.

"Daddy, Daddy," I cried.

He looked at me with a flutter of amusement in his eyes.

"Why did you scream like that?" I asked.

"Honey, that was nothing but a gas ball with nowhere to alight."

He had taken a turn for the worse but was trying hard to retain his sense of humor. It was clear he was failing fast. "I'm calling Dr. Bost. At his home," I said.

Dr. Bost told us to bring Daddy to the hospital. Jonny got rid of the Middleton sisters and went to the garage for the car. I pulled Daddy up and wrapped him in his robe. "Steady does it," I said softly. "We're taking you to the hospital."

The ride to Charleston was long and hot, but Daddy didn't complain once as we bounced over the island roads. We kept all of the windows down so it was too loud to talk—I don't think any of us wanted to in any case. We were lost in our own thoughts.

We pulled up to the emergency entrance at Roper and a nurse met us with a wheelchair. She took him in right away through swinging double doors. Jonny and I urged Mother to follow while we parked the car. We met her up in the room where they had taken Daddy. He was lying flat on the bed when Dr. Bost walked in. The doctor, in a playful gesture, raised his fist and brought it down fast, stopping just before touching Daddy's stomach. None of us thought that was very funny. He felt around Daddy's throat, listened to the stethoscope that he placed on Daddy's chest and back and gently touched the stomach area. When he left the room, Mother, Jonny and I were right behind him. We followed him to the nurses' station and waited until he read the sheets in the file folder.

"Leave him here overnight," Dr. Bost said. "I want to take some tests in the morning."

"It looks bad, doesn't it?" I asked.

Dr. Bost patted me on the shoulder. "Let's hope for the best."

We kissed Daddy goodnight and left for home. It was nearly midnight when we got back home, but I could see Benjamin's truck in the yard before we pulled into the driveway. He must have heard about Daddy and been waiting for me to get home to talk to me about it. Jonny and Mother, as solemn as monks, went inside and I ran for the truck.

"What happened?" Benjamin wanted to know.

"Daddy's back in the hospital."

Benjamin pulled me to him and rested my head on his chest. I was in the place I most wanted, protected by Benjamin, his arms enfolding me.

"I feel I'm embarking on a journey," I choked.

"Whaley, your father is going on a journey. You must face that fact. You cannot go with him. This will be the hardest part of your life. You have to brace for it, meet it face-to-face and go on with your life."

Benjamin was right and I knew it. I thought of Daddy and how he bought me the Baldwin grand and asked me to learn to play "Maria Elena." Charlotte Ann had taught me to play several measures and I was doing fairly well myself in learning to play that piece. I would sit at the piano and play "Maria Elena" if it killed me.

I pulled away from Benjamin. "I'm glad you were here when I got home. I don't mean to be rude, but there is something I must do for Daddy."

"I understand. I'll come back tomorrow."

I flew into the house and played "Maria Elena" late into the night until I could play two lines perfectly. I was thinking that next week when I took my music lesson, I'd ask Charlotte Ann to help me learn to play all of it. That was the only gift I could give Daddy.

I did not go to work the next day but went with Mother to the hospital to pick Daddy up after his tests. Late in the day when we arrived home, I looked around for Benjamin's truck. It was not there. Jonny and I made tomato sandwiches for supper. None of us were hungry. Besides that, a lump in my throat would not go away and it hurt to swallow. Finally I got up and helped clear the table. Standing at the sink washing dishes I saw a strange red car drive into the yard.

Mother looked up. "I don't have the remotest idea who that is. Jonny, can you go out and see what that person in the red car wants?" Jonny flew out of the house but was back in a few seconds.

"The person in that red car wants you," she said to me, grinning coyly.

It was the most dazzling of cars, big and classy, certainly owned by no person known to me. I walked out onto the porch. "Yes?" I called out.

Benjamin crawled out from under the wheel and said, "I came to ask a favor of you?"

I stared open-mouthed. I was too flabbergasted to say anything.

Benjamin walked up to the porch and dragged me by the arms toward the car. I giggled nervously and surveyed him out of the corner of my eye. "A favor?" I finally replied.

He took my hand and dropped two keys on a little chain into it. "Will you drive me around so I can get the feel of your new car?"

"Benjamin! This car is yours?"

"No." He pulled a paper from his pocket. "This is the title, and I believe *your* name is Whaley McLeod."

I stammered and looked up into his eyes. "Benjamin, you didn't."

"I did. It's time you had your own car. Every day I see Mrs. McKinney flying by my store, breaking the Edisto speed limit to get you to work on time. You need your own transportation."

I still couldn't believe it. Was he actually giving me this car?

"Slide in. Take the wheel." Benjamin said.

I got into the driver's seat. Benjamin sat beside me. "I'll never be able to pay you for this kind of car. What kind is it anyway?" I asked.

"A Dodge."

"You understand, Benjamin, I cannot own a Dodge. I'm just not financially able right now…"

He placed his fingers over my mouth and said, "Whaley, I have enough money to buy you a hundred of these cars. It's nothing, really."

I looked up out of the windshield. Mother and Jonny were standing on the front porch, Mother with a look of pure disbelief and Jonny with an enormous grin. I smiled and shrugged sheepishly and Benjamin gave a little wave.

He instructed me how to use the gearshift and we were off. My mind was whirling. What would the islanders think when they saw me driving a luxury car? But moreover, *Where did Benjamin get so much money?*

Early the next morning I called Mrs. McKinney and canceled my seat in her car. When I got home from work that evening, Jonny, Mother and I drove around the island, waving at folks sitting on their porches. Jonny couldn't believe I owned such a beautiful car. Mother couldn't believe Benjamin gave it to me. I could tell she was suspicious of this display of generosity, but she held her tongue. After we'd pulled back into the driveway at home and were walking back up to the house, we turned and glanced back at the car. Jonny laughed and I couldn't help but giggle.

I suddenly realized I wanted to be alone. Separate from Benjamin's company, I didn't care if I never talked with anybody else. I saw a gull on the roof and considered that bird and how satisfied it was. No other sea birds were around, but what did that one care? I wanted to be like that bird, soar away to a quiet place and call forth the solitary ideas in my heart. I desired to open the long-locked folios of my subliminal consciousness and see what really existed. I feigned a headache, took an aspirin, came back to the porch and lay on the glider. Jonny and Mother seemed to notice my sudden wish for anonymity and left me to my own desires. Suddenly, my thoughts plunged into a sea of unspoken words. Where was I in my life? I answered that question quite easily. I was standing at a realization that love was the whole of life and more than all. I was about to lose my child's heart and the man who had inhabited it during my existence. Daddy was going to leave us and what a toll it would take on my heart. Except—yes, except for the new resident of that territory: Benjamin Bodicott. Benjamin had given me a new car, had offered me a home far beyond my wildest dreams, had infused his strength in my head, my hands, my feet, my very soul, just when I thought all things had deserted me. Benjamin was now the man my father had been all those years. He would gently join—he could never replace—Daddy in my heart. I wasn't giving to eternity the man I loved most; my heart was awakening to him. Daddy would be with me always; a heart that has truly loved never forgets. Daddy and Benjamin, in tune with each other, seeking not themselves to please, nor for themselves have any care, but for another give their ease. I could almost hear a foot coming now and the opening of a door. How fortunate could I be? How very blessed.

Chapter Fifteen

After his tests, the doctors at the hospital had said there really wasn't anything more that they could do for Daddy. Dr. Bost gave him some medication for the pain, but said the best thing he could do was rest at home. Mother, Jonny and I took turns caring for him and bringing him soup. He couldn't eat much, and was seeming to get weaker by the day. Mother had set up one of the spare bedrooms on the first floor for him, and he spent most of his time propped up in the bed, sleeping quietly or gazing into some faraway place.

One Sunday after church, Mother and Jonny were in the kitchen preparing dinner. I went to look in on Daddy. I took his hand but he didn't notice. His eyes were settled on something in front of him but I couldn't tell whether it was close or far away.

"Daddy?"

He didn't answer. His eyes, clear and shining, were riveted on something only he could see. He had the most astonished look on his face. He almost couldn't take it in, I believed. Was it real? He appeared to be unsure, and yet he couldn't take his eyes away from whatever it was.

I looked up. Mother was standing in the doorway, twisting a dishtowel in her hands. "Mother, what do you think he is taking in? His eyes…"

"He is seeing what is not to be seen," Mother said, quietly, with a tone of sadness and love I had never heard. Just then Jonny wandered into the room, and began singing from "America the Beautiful":

O beautiful for patriot dream,
That sees beyond the years,
Thine alabaster cities gleam,
Undimmed by human tears.

I felt my own tears beginning to form. Jonny then recited from William Blake:

Who Present, Past and Future sees;
whose ears have heard The Holy Word
That walked among the ancient trees.

Jonny had never been very bookish but on solemn occasions you could depend on her to come through with something eternal, poetic, intelligent. The three of us began to sob like three violins. I felt Daddy's hand stir in mine and I looked up. A calmness had come over his face, a peace I had never seen in him. I knew just then that he had gone. I looked over to Jonny and Mother, and both stared silently back at me. Mother began to slump against the doorframe and Jonny rushed to hold her up.

I looked back toward Daddy. "I never played 'Maria Elena' for you." I sobbed. "You never heard what I could do with the Baldwin grand. I was never at my best for you, but you were always at your best for me." My words were rushing out, sounding more like garbled wails than English words. Finally, I felt someone pulling me away and helping me to the hall. The rest of that day—the rest of that week—seemed a hazy blur to me, pieces of someone else's life that I merely witnessed from behind a gauzy curtain.

All of the islanders, including the wealthy plantation owners, the superintendents of the estates, the cooks and yardmen, the grooms and boatmen, came to the funeral at Heaven's Gate Church. They brought enough food to the house to keep us going for weeks. Mother's two cousins, Shirley and Mag, from Jacksonville, Florida, were there. Mother had called them and told them about Daddy's death. They promised to come and visit again soon after the funeral, as they knew Mother would be lonely.

Mother came to the courthouse the following Monday morning and got Daddy's estate in order. There wasn't very much to be done, but I helped her finish up a few things.

It came to be the pattern that every day when I drove home in my red Dodge, Mother could hardly wait to tell me about Callie and Sallie Middleton, the twins who came to see her every day. "One hooks an arm through this one of mine," Mother explained as she thrust out an elbow, "and the other one hooks an arm through the other one, and all hooked together we walk to the river."

"Why do you think they come every day?" I asked. "We were never close friends."

"I don't know," Mother said. "It *is* curious. I've thought about it. But, you know, I've grown to look forward to their visits. And I think I feel better having taken a lively stroll."

I let it go. If the Middletons were going to pep her up in body and spirit, as they obviously were doing, who was I to object?

After a month or so had passed Cousin Mag and Cousin Shirley came back to visit and stayed with us for a week. They talked about their father, Captain Fletcher Hanson, who was still living in

Jacksonville, and the Clyde Line ships he had taken to Liverpool and Le Havre. Mother wore the gold locket her Uncle Fletch had given her when she was a child and she scrambled around and found a red fez he brought her from Constantinople and a long-handled pipe of marble from another country. They told tales of long ago and of more recent origin, when Uncle Fletch was the captain of the *Shawnee*, the flagship of the Clyde Line's fleet of ships with Indian names, including the *Pawnee*, the *Iroquois* and the *Algonquin*. The *Shawnee* traveled from New York to St. Augustine, stopping in Wilmington and Charleston. Jonny and I heard sea stories for an entire week.

Before Cousin Mag and Cousin Shirley left to go home, they told Mother how very pitiful Uncle Fletch was. "He cannot lie down and sleep," Cousin Shirley said. "He sits up all night, and we worry about him. We stay with him as much as we can, but he still maintains his small house in another part of Jacksonville." Cousin Mag got up enough nerve to ask Mother if she could come to Jacksonville and help out. Mother said that indeed she had been feeling like she needed a change, to get away from the sad memories she kept in Edisto. She promised them that she would come and stay as long as she could. They explained that Uncle Fletch received a good pension from the Clyde-Mallory Line and also had a comfortable savings account. Money was no problem to him. Mother and I talked about her move to Jacksonville to help out. She explained to me that, financially speaking, Uncle Fletch was much better off than she was now that she had no husband. Living in Uncle Fletch's house would reduce her expenses and she believed she would be perfectly comfortable living in her uncle's house and listening to his endless stories of the sea. Besides that, he truly needed some in-house help. According to Mother, no person could have a normal life when they sat up all night. Her cousins couldn't have been happier.

About that time Jonny decided to take over her life and try to make something of it. She got a job teaching school in Myrtle Beach, and suddenly I was left alone in the farmhouse.

I received several letters each week from Mother, telling me how she sat up during the night with Uncle Fletch. They talked about all the "gone on" ones as well as the living. "He has explained to me every hour of light and dark on the sea," she wrote. "It is wonderful. You must hear these stories."

One weekend I drove to Myrtle Beach to visit Jonny. She had taken a room with one of the old families who had guided Myrtle Beach to be the grand strand it had become. They had become like an extended family to Jonny. One night Jonny and I attended a play at the Ocean Forest Hotel, which had been Myrtle Beach's first million-dollar hotel. Some people still called it "the Million Dollar Hotel." It was a wonderful opening night and the actors from New York were professional. Mickey Spillane was in attendance that night. A breakfast was offered after the play and the actors went from table to table, talking with the guests. Jonny and I dined under the famous crystal chandelier as we gazed at the ocean. It was dreamlike.

For that weekend, Jonny and I were like kids again, giggling, shopping in the Arcade at the Ocean Forest Hotel, dining at the Sea Captain's House, walking on the beach. I couldn't remember when I'd had so much fun. Had it not been for my job at the courthouse and my music lessons on Tuesday evenings I would have stayed a few days longer.

I was like a new person as I drove down Highway 17 toward Edisto. My life *was* going to continue no matter what. I would marry Benjamin and have a life of envy. Who else was there who could buy me a red Dodge, build a castle of a house, who knew exactly what he wanted from life and had the wherewithal to get it? There was no one else who had the potential of Benjamin Bodicott. I could be married to anyone else for fifty years and never come close to having a life such as I would live with him. I pondered on whether our finding each other was luck or a blessing. I settled on a blessing, an unqualified blessing and probably undeserved. I hadn't wished for it. I hadn't planned on it. It just happened. Jonny surely would become a matron of Myrtle Beach. Several young men were pursuing her and she liked what she saw. Mother was happy in Jacksonville with Cousin Mag and Cousin Shirley and Uncle Fletch. Daddy's old Plymouth was now in Jacksonville. Cousin Mag did the driving around the city. I doubted Mother would ever want to come back to Edisto Island where she would be nagged by memories. Daddy was gone. Jonny and I would have our own homes. Whatever Mother decided on for her life would be a satisfaction for me. I would help her in any way possible, but at that moment, I was bursting with a desire to see Benjamin and tell him I was ready to plan a wedding. I would not have Daddy for the shoulder so often offered me, and I would miss him. Mother and Jonny would go on to other things. There wasn't anything concerning the wedding that I couldn't do. I still wanted to be married at home, where Charlotte Ann could play the Baldwin grand. When one was married, one's desires in music and other matters should be considered. I wanted to have the usual wedding music played, but somewhere in the lineup "Maria Elena" would find its place, the same as "Clair de lune," my favorite piece forever.

I fairly ran into Benjamin's arms when I got out of my car at the Feed and Seed. "Oh, Benjamin, I want to talk about our wedding. I don't want to put it off much longer."

He looked rather amused, I thought. "Whaley, I've something to show you." He guided me to his truck and we rode over what seemed to be miles and miles of the Old Brothers Place. Then I saw it. The house was in some phase of construction. I couldn't get an idea of the nature of the structure from what I was seeing, but it was huge. Darkness was about to descend upon us and a mist was blowing in from the sea.

Benjamin stopped the truck, then backed up and turned it in a position so that the headlights shined on the foundation taking shape. Leaving the headlights on, we jumped from the truck and ran the rest of the way. Suddenly I stopped running and took in a scene from a magazine or a painting. I didn't think it could be real. A boat was making its way through the marsh. "If that *is* a boat, it looks as though it's moving on marsh grass," I said.

"There's a good, deep inlet there. He's on his way to Florida," said Benjamin.

"And I'm on my way to Heaven," I said. My eyes swept the marsh and darkness of the ocean. I could get only a glimpse of the distant whitecaps tossing themselves this way and that, like dancing girls flipping their skirts. "*Boy.*"

I turned to Benjamin and extended my hand. "I don't believe I've had the pleasure," I said. "I'm the mistress of this estate."

He bowed from the waist. "And I'm the lucky man who is married to the mistress," he said, playing along.

For the better part of the next two hours, Benjamin took me on a tour of the house. "This will be the great hall," he said. "Ceilings fifteen feet high. A curved stairway at the back of the hall will lead to the second floor." Beckoning me to follow, he said, "This will be the dining room."

"I'll have Royal Doulton china, service for twenty-six," I chimed.

He grinned. I couldn't tell if Benjamin thought I was being silly or if he believed I would someday own a service for twenty-six. I didn't know why I said *twenty-six* when I could have said thirty.

"Sunroom." He pointed to a space near the front door.

"Will it be of glass?"

He held up three fingers. "Three walls. Glass. The architect says that room will be your study."

"We don't need a study," I said.

"That's what they call that space—the study. The floors will be hardwood, or oak. That is, except for certain areas such as the porch." Benjamin guided me to the place where the front porch would be. "This is what the architect calls the *Gone With the Wind* porch. There's a grand view from this place but the builder says the view, to him, is of old Edisto Island."

"We'll likely spend a lot of time right here," I said, looking toward the distant marshes. "I'd like a telescope on this porch, please."

"That will be," Benjamin said, with a faint smile on his face. "I would like that."

"We've created a new thrill," I said, imagining the times we would watch ships far away at sea and stars at night.

"Happiness," he answered.

It was in the place where bedroom furniture would one day sit that I had my first thought about all the articles required for use in such a large house. In a fleeting moment I wondered where the furniture for the house would come from. It was a dreadful association of ideas and I didn't know what summoned it to my brain. Mother had needed and used in good measure almost every piece of furniture in our house. Of course I would bring the Baldwin grand, because Daddy said it was mine, but he didn't know how to bring the subject up around Mother and Jonny and neither did I. Mother had *two* daughters, and she was not the kind to disappoint either of them. Jonny was fair and square in most decisions but she never gave the slightest indication that she would give up her share of anything that had belonged to Mother and Daddy. All I new at that moment was that I would have my Baldwin grand with me wherever I went, and I would depend upon Benjamin to go with me to buy the furniture for the new house. I didn't know the source of Benjamin's income and had never been inquisitive about it. He seemed to have a bottomless well of money, and that being the situation, I would simply let him furnish the house.

While I was making momentous decisions, it suddenly occurred to me to ask him the source of his income. "Benjamin?"

"Yes?"

"How did it come to be that you have so much money?" After I said it, I realized I had no business asking him such a personal question. What if he didn't want to divulge the information to me? I quickly added, "You don't have to answer that question, but I have been wondering…"

"It's all right. You know I don't want to spread any rumors around, but you need to know. It's been pressing on my mind."

"It's between us, believe me."

"I'm not halfway to knowing how much I've got, but a banker in Georgia keeps up with it."

"How much do you have?" I asked.

"I just told you, I don't know that."

"Where did you get it?"

"My parents and some relatives decided to buy an island and fix it up as a resort."

"They are dead," I said, trying to help him out.

Benjamin nodded his head. "They're dead all right."

I looked at him expectantly. I didn't want to pry, but I knew there was much more to the story. Benjamin took a deep breath and blew his cheeks into small balloons. He exhaled slowly and said, "We all worked hard, very hard. From sunup to sundown. Finally it was done. The island? She was a beauty. Mother was dead and my father could barely walk. I tried to carry the load. My uncle decided to sell the island and we got a sack of money."

"A sack? Like the ones the fertilizer comes in?"

"No. There was no sack. The money was in the bank, and most of mine is still there."

"Your money came from the sale of the island?"

"That's about the size of it. My part, which included my mother's part and my father's part, came to more than I want to admit. My father was the architect of the island but my hands finished it." Benjamin looked at me as if to determine whether or not I was taking all of it in. I wanted to urge him on, to hear the rest of the story, but I could see that he was in misery as he tried to explain something he himself didn't fully understand.

"You see, Whaley, I'm not the kind of person who likes to be rich. Rich folks don't interest me. I'm just a plain Joe. I would like to live within my means, but I don't know what my means amount to. The money has been a burden to me." He paused for a moment then added, "What I really want is peace. Contentment. I can be content on what I make at the Feed and Seed and that's all I want, except for my house. My parents worked all the time, daylight and dark. We were not a family. I want a big house, a fine house really, some children, a warm fireplace, a home."

"And that is what you will have, right here." I pointed to the foundation of Benjamin's house-in-progress. Suddenly we heard a siren in the distance. We watched as the red lights flew by on the distant road. After the emergency vehicle passed by, it seemed as if a burden had been lifted. I knew as much as I wanted to know about my beloved's inheritance. Some day, after I knew more, I would learn the particulars and see that it was protected for Benjamin and our children.

We moved on to another space. The truck headlights were now dim and flickering. Benjamin was not a person who could describe things from his heart, jabber and make small talk. Benjamin only talked when he had something to say. As we wandered about, he was talkative, but he wasn't a person who could express his longings, yearnings, his happiness and, probably, grief. In every other virtue, nothing could surpass him. I could live with that, I believed. I was a gabber already and we didn't need two of those in the family. Just then I realized he could be as deep-mouthed as a bird dog.

Looking away from the area in which we stood, perhaps far away into some vista I would never understand, he uttered, "If collaborators persistently and unforgettably in nominations of meticulously frustrating responsibility with unalterable determination regarding architecture, tapestry and porcelain begat the celebration of illuminations forevermore, happiness would bestow its blessings."

I puzzled at him, trying to put together his words. "Benjamin, I've been thinking: every once in a while your vocabulary startles me. You speak in terms that the orators of England used, and your voice is as soft as ashes. Your vocal cords must be wrapped in satin. How did you accumulate such a talent?"

He shrugged. "I preserved some of the words used by the people who lived near us, and a lot of the verbiage of my father and mother and my mother's brothers and their families. I picked it up. Every word may not be in the right place but I know what I'm saying."

I let it go at that.

Chapter Sixteen

*I*f there is a single trait common to all Edisto Islanders it's
their love of their land on the island and their unwillingness
to sell it. I never desired to become a *grande dame* and one of the
richest women on South Carolina's coast but as the days passed I
came to believe I would be one of them whether I desired it or not.
A blue blood had so much to live up to. They were criticized and
degraded, usually because of jealousy, and there wasn't much they
could do about it. I wondered what it would be like to be married
to a man of means. As I thought about it, I would just have to learn
how to be a woman of means. I made a mental list of the things
that would be expected of such a person. In order to fit the mold,
I worked harder on my music lessons, sitting at the Baldwin grand
and trying to learn several pieces by heart, as they say. It would be
likely that I would be asked to play the piano on certain occasions,
perhaps when I entertained the other families from the island in
our grand estate.

I worked harder at my job at the courthouse and took on the
goal of one day, perhaps, being given the job of court clerk. I
liked to go to the courtroom, which I did almost every day, and
sometimes, when an interesting case was being tried, I ran down a
hallway and slipped around two corners to the dark little doorway
that few people knew existed. I could quietly step inside and
watch and listen to what was happening in the courtroom. No
person could see me standing in the darkness of the tiny balcony.
I didn't tell anybody where I was going or where they could find

me. I watched and listened to Vestal and tried to remember his countenance and vocabulary and manner of moving and how he dealt with plaintiffs, defendants, judges and lawyers. I discovered this hiding place one day when I was sent to the courtroom and took a wrong turn; I burst onto the place that would become my secret hideaway. It was my hush-hush place, the location where I learned all I could of what Vestal and the other employees of the court did in the hallowed courtroom. I gave my little isolated room a name—Holy of Holies—and no other person knew the name or that I went there.

Chapter Seventeen

The first of the cool weather came toward the middle of October. Construction of Benjamin's "castle in the sand" (that's what I privately called it) was going well. It was beginning to look like a residence, a mansion really, and I could mentally place a few pieces of furniture where I would want it. Mother had returned from Jacksonville for a week on the island. It seemed that every conversation we had from the moment she stepped off the bus and got settled in at home began with, "The Middleton twins came today. They locked their arms in mine and we had a strenuous walk to the river." I was sick of hearing about Callie and Sallie, didn't have the faintest idea what they were up to or talked about and couldn't care less. I had to admit, though, that the name Middleton stood for a lot in the South Carolina Lowcountry. The Middletons had bought good property, planted extraordinary gardens and raised bright children (even if some of them did insist on dressing alike well into their adult years). They were more than aristocrats; if there had been any South Carolina royalty, they would have been it.

One day I changed the subject and told Mother that Benjamin and I would be married soon. I hadn't planned on telling her about my plans yet and I didn't want to bring Jonny in on it, but the time was coming when I would have to start planning my wedding.

"I've always thought the two of you, as a couple, look wonderful together," Mother said. "That's important. Perhaps not as important as some other traits or characteristics, but it is significant nevertheless. I think he will be a good provider of all that you need, and if that should not prove to be true, you are self-supporting. I'm not worried about you."

"Do you like him? I mean, will he fit in with our family, do you think?"

"He seems to fit in with every situation that I've noticed. He is friendly to all, neat and clean and is willing to do anything to help. Have you discussed where you will live?"

"Benjamin is in the process of building a home. He bought the Old Brothers Place, and the house will sit back from the marsh, on a ridge of large oak trees. He went to Savannah and signed a contract with a builder who is well known for his construction of large homes. He remodeled and updated some of the noted homes in the squares. I've met the contractor one time. He's a pro. Knows just everything about brick and stone and marble and porcelain and all of that. I would trust him to do a good job."

Mother smiled.

"Oh, sometimes I don't know," I went on. "It's a huge house, like one the Kennedys or the Hollywood people might own. I'll have to adjust to it."

"Does he have any trappings to add to it, such as portraits of his ancestors?"

I knew Mother didn't like the trappings of the aristocracy, as she called portraits, cut glass and the like. "Oh heavens no. We'll have to buy everything from scratch."

"You've always had good taste, Whaley. *Very* good taste. I think you've made a fair decision in selecting a husband and your house will be outstanding."

"Please don't tell Jonny," I urged. "I'll tell her very soon, when I get a day or two off and go to Myrtle Beach."

Mother took a deep breath and rolled her eyes. "What do you think about Jonny? Is she happy in Myrtle Beach?"

"Very happy. She's settled down more than anyone I know. She likes the school on Oak Street and her students adore her. She's learning to play golf."

Mother looked a little weary, I thought.

"You did good, Mummy," I said, deferring to the name I called her when I was a child. "Jonny and I are going to turn out the way you wanted, and the way Daddy would have liked. I promise."

Jonny came for a couple of days at Thanksgiving and seemed a little edgy to get back to Myrtle Beach. Mother had gone back to Jacksonville the day before Jonny's arrival. Mother and I had cooked a turkey and dressing and a couple of pies. Benjamin made himself a little scarce over the holiday, or so I thought. I finally decided that he was giving me some time alone with my family. It didn't feel right to talk about getting married. Not just then. There would be a time when Jonny and I would be just sisters, exploring our dreams for the future. That would be the time. She knew Benjamin and I were close and she wouldn't be surprised when she got the official word. She was in and out before I knew it and I was back in the turmoil of a Monday at the courthouse. It had become my practice on that kind of day to sit at my desk and work quietly until after 9:30, when the court clerks were in the courtrooms and everything had quieted down. I rarely looked at the court dockets and knew little of the cases being tried, but if I kept up with my plans to seek a job as a court clerk, it would be necessary to learn everything to do a good job.

Just before lunch, Judge Parker showed up at my desk. "Whaley, could I prevail upon you to type a letter for me?"

"Yes, sir."

"I've written the letter in longhand. It's in the folder with some of my letterhead stationery and an envelope. If you'll type what I've written, including addressing the envelope, then please bring it to the courtroom this afternoon and hand it to my clerk."

"It's a pleasure, Judge Parker. I'll bring the letter to the courtroom this afternoon." He smiled, gave me a pat on the back and left the vault.

Around lunchtime, my friend from the tax office, Hannah Vanderhorst, met me in the hallway and we walked to the place where we ate lunch almost every day. We called it the hole-in-the-wall. Hannah lived with her sister, Julia, and her mother, Josephine, in a huge old home on Tradd Street in Charleston, where I had visited. Hannah and I had become close over our daily lunches and we occasionally shared secrets with each other. I treasured my friendship with the entire family. She knew nothing of Benjamin or my relationship with him but had confided in me that she believed she was in love with a man who worked for the City of Charleston. She would be one of the first people I would entrust with the knowledge of my upcoming marriage to Benjamin when I felt the time was right for the big announcement. I realized I must tell her very soon. Sometimes I pictured what character her face would take when I told her my biggest secret.

We ambled on several streets as we made our way back to the courthouse. My workload that day was a little lighter than usual. I planned to take my afternoon break in the Holy of Holies, after I delivered Judge Parker's letter to his clerk. Hannah knew nothing of the Holy of Holies or the goal I had set for myself to someday work in the courtroom.

I typed Judge Parker's letter quickly, addressed the envelope, placed both in a file folder and hurried to the courtroom. From a corner of my eye I could see that a man was sitting in the defendant's chair. What an awful place to be, I thought. A lawsuit against a person was bad enough, but to be sitting before a courtroom filled with people and be questioned to the very bottom of your soul and under oath was something I could not possibly imagine. My back was to the defendant, and I was glad of that. Judge Parker saw me hand the folder to his clerk and nodded his head. A faint smile crossed his lips. I was thinking how much I admired Judge Parker for his fairness and courtesy as well as his expertise in the judge's chair. At that moment a very familiar voice fell on my ears. Suddenly I realized it was Benjamin's voice. Without the slightest thought of self-preservation I turned to look at the defendant—Benjamin.

He wore tan trousers, a white shirt and green tie. His jacket looked to be of worsted wool. His hair was meticulously groomed and his shoes shined like mirrors. My heart gave a leap and I quickly turned back around and made a slow move toward the door. I took my time, as I wanted to understand what was going on. My attention was suddenly taken by the questioning attorney. It seemed Benjamin was being cross-examined by the lawyer for the plaintiff. He hadn't seen me and I turned and flew from the courtroom as fast as I could move without attracting any notice. Back in the hallway I broke into a run for the Holy of Holies.

No other person in the entire world knew where I was at that moment. How dizzy I was as I cast my eyes down on the scene in the courtroom. What was this trial about? Why had Benjamin been brought to court? I held onto the fragile railing for support.

Obviously the beginning questions to serve the advantage of the transcript had been asked and other questioning had taken place before I accidentally fell into the scenario.

"Now, Mr. Bodicott, would you please describe your working procedure to the court."

"For the past five years or so I've owned the Feed and Seed. I sell fertilizer and Mr. Butler is one of my suppliers. I pay him for the fertilizer he provides me and I sell the product for a profit."

Good for you, Benjamin, I almost called down from the Holy of Holies. He spoke more distinctly and with better sense than I had ever heard him. He could speak in clear terms if he had to. Benjamin was an honest and wise man. From his answer I came to the conclusion that someone named Mr. Butler had brought him to court and claimed he had defaulted on a payment.

"And how successful are you, Mr. Bodicott, in selling the bags of fertilizer that arrive from Mr. Butler's warehouse?"

"Objection! The question is irrelevant," barked Benjamin's lawyer. I recognized him as Otis Wiley.

Before Judge Parker had an opportunity to rule on the objection, Benjamin said, "There may be a linguistic or temperamental affinity to the belief that the day one serves as the parliamentary representation for this country, the advisability of sending assimilating particulars inevitably takes us to perplexing righteousness of its cause in order to enable us to prevail."

"Mr. Bodicott," Judge Parker interrupted, "between the idea and the reality of what you said may dwell caverns and cisterns of information regarding profit and loss, but I am at a total loss to figure it out. You said your piece with a bang, not a whimper, and I credit you with having some knowledge of the information you strived to impart. I'm going to overrule the question as being irrelevant because I suppose you have already answered it. Overruled."

"Mr. Bodicott, I'm asking you very simply if you ever deposited a check made to the 'Feed and Seed' or to 'Bodicott's Fertilizer Company'?" the lawyer asked.

"I deposit checks every week," Benjamin answered.

I began to feel weak and weary and my hand shook involuntarily as though it had a kind of palsy. No longer could I listen to the testimony of Benjamin as a witness in a lawsuit against him. I left the Holy of Holies and flew back to my desk. Mr. Lyon walked in about the time I dissolved into my chair. "I've been in the courtroom," I said too quickly, though not altogether lying. "Had a little work for Judge Parker."

"We expect you to take care of Judge Parker's typing when he asks you. Keep up the good work, Whaley." Mr. Lyon walked farther into the vault and asked for a copy of Doreen Wisby's will. I watched Mr. Lyon. He bought my explanation in the blink of an eye and was engrossed in another matter. Although I could not stand to listen to Benjamin's testimony, I realized I couldn't go through *not* hearing it. I hurried back to the Holy of Holies.

The testimony had taken a turn.

"Mr. Bodicott, with due respect to the outpouring of many-syllabled words, it's my belief that you have a very limited vocabulary," the lawyer for the plaintiff said.

Oh my mercy. *Where was the lawyer going with this?* I wondered.

Benjamin said nothing.

"Mr. Bodicott, where did you go to school?"

"I did not attend school," Benjamin answered softly.

I always worried about *something*, something I didn't know about, a characteristic that was different from the rest of us. Now I knew what it was. *Benjamin never went to school.*

"Mr. Bodicott, you never set foot in a schoolhouse, did you?" the lawyer queried.

"No, sir."

Judge Parker interrupted. "Mr. Bodicott, no one is trying to embarrass you here. I believe it is the law of the land that all children attend school. Will you tell us where you went to school?"

"I did not attend school, your honor."

"How did it come about that you never attended school?" the judge asked. "Did you live in hibernation?"

"No, your honor."

"Would you explain to the court how you evaded going to school all these years?"

"My father and my mother's two brothers and their families came to America from the island of Tasmania, south of Australia."

Benjamin paused, and the judge said, "Go on. I want to hear this, but I don't necessarily want my grandchildren to know about it." Laughter filled the courtroom and the judge lifted his gavel and brought it down to indicate he expected quietness to prevail.

"Your honor, the three families had enough assets to buy Whiteswamp Island, off the coast of Georgia, near St. Marys. The island later was named Corkery Island. My mother was a Corkery before marriage. The Bodicotts and the Corkerys came from Tasmania on three large vessels, carrying workers and materials. The idea was to build a recreational facility second to none in the world. It was supposed to be a sort of Garden of Eden; a place where the world's wealthy people could go and enjoy beauty and privacy."

"I think Corkery Island has turned out to be just that," the judge remarked. "I've been there. It truly is one of the world's beauty spots."

"It was sold to the Kuwaitis seven years ago, for two hundred and eighty-five million dollars," Benjamin explained. "To answer your question, there was no boat to be used as a school boat. I was the only child on the island. I never went to school."

The judge continued. "Mr. Bodicott, this is an amazing story. I'm intrigued with it and with you. You have to be a person of some resilience to have no schooling and end up with millions of dollars."

"Yes, your honor, I'm blessed with many millions of dollars."

The judge motioned for the lawyer to pick up the questioning. "Mr. Bodicott, can you write any words?"

"I can write my name and the name of my company."

"How did you learn to do that?" the lawyer asked.

"A man wrote my name and the name of my company on a piece of paper. With a pencil, I traced it thousands and thousands of times, and now I can write smoothly and quickly."

I gasped loudly before I thought to slap a hand across my mouth. Daddy had written Benjamin's name and the name of the Feed and Seed on paper. It was *Daddy's* writing that Benjamin had traced thousands of times. When Benjamin wrote those names on any document, it was Daddy's style of writing. I shrunk back in the shadows but apparently no one had heard me.

"You cannot read?"

"No, sir. But I believe it is better not to be able to read and write than not to be able to do something else." The lawyer ignored the remark and asked about Benjamin's system of mathematics. I decided to leave—I couldn't take any more surprises.

My spirit was weak and weighed heavily on me when I slipped into the hallway. In one day my life had changed drastically. I arrived at the courthouse that morning having everything—a new car, a man waiting to become my husband, a good job, robust health, a mansion on Edisto Island—and now it seemed I had nothing. I had lost a home, a husband, a soul mate, a life. Who could marry a man who could not read the books you loved and discuss them with you on long walks on star-studded evenings? Who could marry a man who could never write you a love note to keep in a treasured place?

My mind was whirling. I absentmindedly finished some typing and tidied my desk while I kept an eye out for Vestal. I would wait until he came back to his desk if it took until ten o'clock that night. I had to find out what happened.

At five o'clock the office staff began to leave. Mr. Lyon, Mrs. Lingle and Mrs. Moffitt were finishing up when Vestal came running into the office, his arms loaded with file folders. I walked toward Mr. Lyon's desk, and pretended to amble over to Vestal as an afterthought.

"Vestal?"

"Whaley, I saw you in the courtroom this afternoon."

"I was delivering some work for Judge Parker." I tried my best to keep my voice steady. "Oh, by the way, I overheard a little of a most unusual court case. What happened regarding that man who never went to school?"

Vestal didn't hesitate a second. "That man is a curiosity. He's handsome, wealthy, likeable and successful and yet, he never went to school. But he had a good reason. He lived on an island and there was no transportation to the mainland. There still is no bridge to Corkery Island but you can get there by boat from St. Marys, Georgia, or Fernandina Beach, Florida. I'll bet, when all is said and done, he knows more than a lot of people who hold college degrees."

"What was he tried for?" Even though I knew the answer, I didn't want Vestal to know how much I had overheard.

"Fraudulent bookkeeping. But Judge Parker threw it out of

court. The plaintiff had no case against the defendant. He was being tried for a crime he didn't commit. It all came down to the system of bookkeeping. No one could understand this man's structure when dealing with numbers but him. There was no liability, no dishonesty, nothing of responsibility for which to hold him. He's a free man. Judge Parker actually apologized to him for the unfortunate ordeal."

He looked at me and shrugged. I tried to smile nonchalantly. Vestal began to sort his files and I left quickly.

My mind was hammering, telling me that Benjamin was innocent of any charges against him. He did not steal any money to buy my car. He could indeed buy me a hundred red Dodges if I desired. He was a man of integrity, humility and extraordinary good looks. But he was uneducated. This was something I could not overlook. All things considered, I could not marry him.

Chapter Eighteen

The month that followed was one of squandered courting. Every word that came from Benjamin's mouth was in anticipation of the moment when we said, "I do." My conversation skills were on vacation. If I could think of the right thing to say, I couldn't utter it. I could have been reading a timetable or a catalog and benefited more than from any conversation we had.

Benjamin didn't know that I knew anything about his appearance at the courthouse. I didn't want to break his heart. His upbringing was done and could not be changed. *I* could not be changed. I was Southern to the marrow of my bones. Never in the world would I hurt Benjamin if I could find another way to tell him that our wedding was off. Perhaps I could say we'd put things "on hold."

I didn't know which laws held and which ones didn't. There were laws of propriety, laws of God, laws of the state, laws of the Constitution of the country and a hundred other laws. Kipling said there was a law of the jungle—Surely the weak shall perish and only the fit survive: the wolf that shall keep it may prosper, but the wolf that shall break it must die. What kind of wolf was I?

The next Friday a car pulled into the front yard just as I put the last touch of dressing on my salad. Jonny stuck her head in the front door. "Is the pianist *appassionato* around?"

I hoo-hooed from the kitchen. Jonny went down the hall, threw her suitcase on the bed and came into the kitchen. "What's up?"

I pulled out a plate for her and put it on the table. "I've a lot to talk over. You're in for a big surprise if you're still a romantic who thinks nothing's changed in the last dozen years."

She took a big bite of tomato and lettuce. "So?"

"Listen. There're some things I haven't told you. I only told Mother about it recently."

"What are you talking about?"

"Do you remember Benjamin Bodicott? The man who owns the Feed and Seed and a lot of other land?"

"I don't know about all the *other* land."

"Well, to make a long story a shorter one, we're engaged to be married." I said.

"What? You have to be kidding."

"I'm not kidding. He bought the Old Brothers Place and is building a house to die for. He wants a house with a beautiful design, you know what I mean, with acanthus leaves on the Corinthian columns and a lily pool surrounded by statues."

"Where's the money coming from?"

"He's loaded. I mean *really* loaded. I'll tell you about that later, but now, just believe everything I tell you, although you'll think I've lost my senses."

"Yep. You said it."

"His house is under construction. The plan is for us to marry here in Mother's house and live in his mansion."

"I think I could do that."

"Well, I can't."

"Why?"

"Because he never went to school. What would the islanders think of me?" I asked.

"For one thing, what do you care what they say as long as you

122

have a good man and live in a mansion? And by the way, *everybody* is required to go to school."

I pushed my plate back. Any appetite I thought I had was gone. "He was raised on an island, off the coast of Georgia. The Kuwaitis bought the island for millions of dollars and the Bodicotts were as rich as Doris Duke. Maybe richer. Even so, there wasn't a school boat to transport him, the only child on the island, to the mainland. He never went to school. You go and figure. He can't put three sentences together right, and sometimes he blurts out three-, four- and five-syllable words that make no sense to anyone but him."

Jonny paused for a second. "Does Mother know any of this?"

"Only that Benjamin is very well off and that we plan to marry, but that's what I want to talk to you about; I'm *not* going to marry him, but he doesn't know it yet."

"Would he consider *me?*"

"Shut up, Jonny. You don't want him any more than I do."

"Speak for yourself. I didn't like school either."

I looked my sister straight in the eyes. "Listen. Get serious. You're my shrink and I need some good, solid advice. I'm in trouble up to my armpits. If I hadn't invited him to come hear Mr. DeShazo play the piano none of this would've happened."

"Who's Mr. DeShazo?"

"The man who delivered the Baldwin grand. I invited the island folks to come hear Mr. DeShazo play the piano and Benjamin came, and since that night he's been smitten."

"I hear of worse things every day of my life."

"You don't, Jonny. Benjamin never set a foot in a schoolroom. How's that for husband and father material?"

"He's not an axe murderer."

"I'm serious. I don't know how to handle all of this. You've got to help me or I'm going to crash."

"You're not serious."

"I am serious, and you're the only person who can save me."

Jonny got up and walked around the room. I assumed she was giving some heavy thought to my problem while a finger was curling a lock of hair at the nape of her neck.

"I think you're making a fool of yourself. It's something like planting a kumquat tree on Edisto Island. The tree might live and it might not, but what has school got to do with it? You would not fall in love with a dimwit. Benjamin is smart, and your children will become a John F. Kennedy or an Adlai Stevenson."

This conversation did not lend itself to planting kumquat trees, I was thinking. Jonny didn't get it. She was going to be of no help to me. I suggested we sleep in the same bed that night. If we could discuss the matter until the threshold of first light, we might come to a conclusion.

Chapter Nineteen

$\mathcal{I}$ had never dreamed of such a thing, but Jonny McLeod was a psychologist without a nurse, a secretary, an office, a recliner or a medical library. When I told her that, she said she did have a portfolio. I knew she was kidding and began my dissertation with Benjamin telling me where his mother is buried and my thought that he would ask me to marry him. From there I went into the courtroom scene and the astounding revelation that Benjamin had never gone to school. Jonny listened but I could tell she was restless. I went to the closet and got more pillows. She propped two at her back and I put one under my knees. When we were truly comfortable she got down to the brass tacks of the matter.

"Proposition number one," Jonny said, "we have to decide who Benjamin Bodicott is." Without pausing, she went into her composite of him. "He owns a company. There are no stockholders because he holds no stock. We don't know what office equipment he has because we don't know if he has an office, but he has assembled his own methods for keeping his books. We know he is honest because Judge Parker deemed him that. There is no concealment such as a worm in the bud, because everything was laid bare in the courtroom and nothing was found to be contrary to the norm. Right?"

"Right."

"As far as an American capitalistic enterprise is concerned, we know that Benjamin Bodicott is a success and he has the ability to bear it with humility. So rare a man."

"Up to now, Benjamin is honest, has no concealment and is rich," I reiterated.

"Right. *I* could take him on those qualities alone, but let's go further. Benjamin owns a thriving business that is in no danger of winning a government contract. He alone makes up the board of trustees. Should something have to be voted upon, he can put his feet upon his desk, pause, remove his feet and declare that the board has come to a decision." Jonny turned and looked at me as she added, "It's a small business but you can't beat the partnership."

"It sounds good, Jonny, but you haven't come to the main issue, the school part."

Johnny held up a hand. "I'm coming to that. If we're going to weigh the product, we have to consider every part of it."

"Go ahead." I knew where she was going. Benjamin was near perfect, except for the one thing I could not accept.

"Okay, he's honest, has no concealment, is rich and is successful in his business." Jonny gathered her knees up and clasped her hands around them. "We've established who he is and we know that his business is in good shape as long as the people on Edisto plant their fields, and that will go on until doomsday. Leaping ahead, we'll take a look at the future, parenthetically."

I slapped a leg. "Proceed."

"I'm looking at Benjamin as if he's not married to you or anyone else. This scenario is sometime in the future. The harmonious connection between Benjamin and the islanders continues. They like him for who he is and how his business affords a pleasant rapport. Neither will intimidate the other regardless of education pursuits or the lack thereof. In the island world, where a clever businessman isn't born every minute, there is no lording it over another. Benjamin has endured the test of time and has a sense of who he is, regardless of his wealth or intelligence. He and the islanders, including the wealthy Northerners who bought the plantations, realize that many people who have achieved a proper education never do the things they should do. A man's training begins with his mother. He learns his first lesson there and takes the banner into a mature life. Benjamin Bodicott is centered well in his skin and others realize it. He is achieving his goals while he is young enough to enjoy them. He begins his day by lacing up his boots for vigorous selling and heavy lifting. His home will be a place where superficial and veneer are rarely mistaken for reality and profoundness. I've noticed that he can accept a compliment without changing the subject to his flaws."

"And so?" I query.

"Look at the name-droppers. The flip side of the big name is a considerable insecurity. The landmarks on Benjamin's route to security are not the flashiest cars on the island. He drives a truck. He hasn't a boat when in reality he could hold the wheel of a schooner or travel in a private railroad car. Benjamin is a man of integrity but not harsh, neither is he warm and cuddly. He is open and friendly."

Jonny paused and I believed she had finished her homily, but she was just getting started. "Let us consider a future in which you are married to Benjamin Bodicott. You, Whaley, must guard against trivial comments and shallow remarks fueled by jealousy. Some will give their stamp of approval selfishly. Your ego is of primary consideration. You will be faced with dealing with those who have preconceived ideas about many subjects, including one's education. Must you accept their views, or not? While you hold nothing against them, once you *were* one of them. Can you keep your mold, your cast, steady and hard?"

"Wait," I called out. "You're getting too close to the subject. My heart is pounding."

"I was hoping it would. We're now at the heart of the matter. Let's assume you belong to Benjamin and he is yours. You are a celebrated couple, not only for your wealth but also for your philanthropy, doled out in myriad ways. Everyone will love both of you, as well as your children. You will help the islanders and others when a hurricane makes landfall on a high tide and the destruction from the surge of wind-driven water is a phenomenon. It will be you, Whaley, on whom the islanders will call when tutoring is necessary, and it will be Benjamin's call when tuition money is nonexistent.

"Listen, Sister, this likely is the most complex portion of your life. Education comes in many forms. What greater wisdom is there than an act of good will? The mistake would be to not accept Benjamin's proposal and never to live in one of the great houses of the Lowcountry. Marry him. Be happy. Raise your children with pride and educate them with exaltation. They will be exceptional. Benjamin Bodicott is a prize awarded to you. He is a gift from God. Accept him admirably and proudly."

Two nights later I was lying alone on my bed and my mind rattled with all that Jonny had told me. She was right, of course, but my courage was weak. Who was it who said worry is the interest paid by those who borrow trouble? Some of the old sayings had credence. Hagar, a woman who rendered maid services on Edisto Island, frequently said, "Never trouble trouble 'til trouble troubles you."

It required all my tactics of whim, tendency and resentment to focus my attention on a life with Benjamin, a man who never went to school. If I decided to marry him, my outlook would be changed forever. I would never in my entire life beam my energy on Benjamin's lack of an education, which lay at the core of his history, but I would adopt a different viewpoint and renewed energy. The central point of my attention, as Jonny pointed out, would be that Benjamin's lack of schooling was counterbalanced by honesty, loyalty, perseverance and other accessories of his make-up. Should any part of our lives come under scrutiny that was unbearable, it wouldn't last long. Nasty speculation never did. It always died down. Benjamin would be accepted for the fine man he is. For me, though, everything was a disaster, like the aftermath of a hurricane when the Edisto River flooded and drowned the young corn. The planters were good people and they went to work replanting, immediately. I had to replant my mind from the washout it had suffered. It would take some time, but I hoped I could work the soil.

✳

Chapter Twenty

On Tuesday, I noticed Benjamin's truck following my red Dodge when I pulled up to the house.

"Hi there!" he said, getting out.

"I'm going to run in and get my music book. Would you like to go to the Kells' dairy farm with me? You won't have to listen in on all the wrong notes I'll play."

"Sounds great. Think you could put up with the truck?"

"Sure."

When I came back Benjamin was dusting off my seat. "It's not the red Dodge but it'll do," he said.

I had a sneaky feeling that after I had taken my music lesson we would ride to the new house. Benjamin was more comfortable in his truck while driving on the unpaved road.

Mrs. Kell was tending a flowerbed when she saw us. She came to the truck. "Why Benjamin, I didn't expect to see you. What a pleasure." I didn't know the Kells knew him that well, but then again, everyone in the region bought their fertilizer and seeds from Benjamin. She took us to the patio and left quickly, saying she would return with some lemonade. When she came back, Benjamin was having the time of his life examining the different kinds of shrubs in the yard. Charlotte Ann came to the porch and motioned for me to come in. Carrying the Shirmer book, off I went, leaving Benjamin and Mrs. Kell discussing the landscape architecture.

"Whaley, the recital has been set for May. Which of the pieces you are learning do you want to play?"

"If I played 'Maria Elena,' would it be compatible with the other pieces to be played in the recital?"

Charlotte Ann thought for a moment. "I think 'Maria Elena' would be wonderful, and we'll let you tell the audience that it was your father's favorite piece."

"Thank you, Charlotte Ann. I'll practice it to death and you will be proud of me."

"I'm already proud of you, Whaley."

As I opened the Shirmer book and began to play the piece I had practiced that week, I was thinking about the recital. I hadn't given a thought to getting a dress for the occasion, but I would take care of that very soon. Charlotte Ann stood behind me, saying, "one-and-two-and-three-and-four-and…"

When the lesson was finished, Benjamin and Mrs. Kell were still sitting on the patio talking about plants. He seemed in no hurry to leave. "I was born on Corkery Island," he was saying.

"That's off the coast of Georgia, I believe. We spent the night there once, when we were on our way to Florida?" Mrs. Kell said, though it sounded as if she was asking Benjamin if it were true.

"Originally it was Whiteswamp Island and later it was named after my mother's family, the Corkerys. My mother's family were from Tasmania Island."

"Who landscaped Corkery Island so beautifully?" Mrs. Kell asked.

"I worked hard at planting flowers among the palmettos and wax myrtle bushes. It was years before the landscaping was finished. It was hard. There must have been a million wild boars on the island."

"Today it is one of the world's beauty spots, and I'm glad one can get there by boat from St. Marys, Georgia."

"Thank you, Mrs. Kell. I don't get down there much these days. I want to go soon and look over the cemetery where my mother is buried."

"I believe your family sold the island?"

"We sold it to the Kuwaitis. My family died out and I inherited the assets."

Mrs. Kell looked around at me. "I'm glad you and Whaley are friends. Whaley is one of Edisto's finest young women."

"She is," Benjamin answered. He asked me if we were ready to go and I nodded. We held hands as we went back to the truck.

Chapter Twenty-one

*B*enjamin turned into the driveway of the house-in-making. "It's amazing how much the house changes each time I see it," I said as we rounded the last curve. "And so much of it is stone, which is absolutely beautiful. I never dreamed…"

"Winnsboro blue granite, from Winnsboro, in the midlands. The State House is made of the same."

"It's a stone mansion—I mean, really. I cannot believe it."

"What did you expect?"

"I don't know, but this is far beyond my expectations, my dreams. It's a castle."

"Come inside," he said.

It was the first time I had seen the house since the roof was installed. There was a kind of comfort and privacy emanating from the rooms. As we walked on I realized that each room was separate and I could get a more accurate feel for the finished product. We stopped in the sunroom. It had three walls of glass. I could picture it with green plants extending nearly to the ceiling and a beautiful light fixture. I could envision that room being outstanding from the inside as well as from outside the house. It would be my favorite, surely. Benjamin took me into the kitchen to see the marble floor. It wasn't completely dark but he got down on his knees and shined a flashlight on the veins in the stone. It appeared to be a beige background with saffron veins. I didn't think I had ever seen such a beautiful kitchen floor. It was magnificent.

"The sink will be here," Benjamin said, taking me in his arms and swinging me around to the window space. We waltzed around the room and went right out the doorway onto a porch area. The sun was going down. "The sea and the moon are one," Benjamin said.

"What do you mean?"

"When the moon rises, it and the sea are one blaze of red. Not for long, though."

I could not remember a single time when I had watched the moon rise on the horizon. I had seen the ribbon of moonlight on the sea a hundred times and more and I had focused on globs of moonlight tossed upon the stormy seas, but I had never taken the time to gaze at the first gleam that rose above the water. "What a spectacle it must be to sit at this place and watch the moon rise above the sea," I said. "I can't wait to see that."

As I kissed Benjamin, I was thinking how very happy he was and I hoped everything the future held for us would make him as happy as he was tonight. I was thrilled with the prospects of the future and just bowled over by the beauty of the house, but not deliriously so as he was. As I thought about it, we made a curious couple—Will Rogers and Amelia Earhart. He was so grounded in who he was and that was that. I was forever in the clouds, taking on my next endeavor.

"Benjamin?"

"What is it, honey?"

"I was just thinking. We're quite different."

"How so?"

"Your people were wealthy and mine were working people. There's a huge difference. I'm not complaining, but there *is* a difference. My father was a farmer. Some years he made more than expected. Other years, when the weather didn't cooperate, he had to fall back on his nest egg to pay the taxes. Your father owned a famous resort and raked in millions of dollars. As a young man you came into a fortune. Looking at my situation, the only thing I can count on is the Baldwin grand. Daddy always said it was mine, but that's all he promised. We're from different backgrounds, different circumstances. Will that make a difference?"

Benjamin took a deep breath. "Every man creates his fortune. What is *fortune*, anyway? Your father was a farmer, and yet…"

"Yet, what?" Benjamin seemed to have stopped in mid-thought. I didn't know if he would continue his explanation.

"And yet," he began again, "your father and you, Whaley, and almost everybody else has a fortune that I do not have. I would give…"

"Stop," I said as I grabbed his arm. Benjamin seemed on the verge of telling me he had no education and I didn't want to hear that. His lack of an education was a cross he would have to bear forever, but nothing would be gained by talking about it, trying to explain it. I had finally begun to see that his traits and characteristics far outweighed any doctorate that was ever earned in any of the institutions of higher learning in the world. Benjamin's qualities and attributes couldn't be summed up in degrees from colleges. I could think of a few people who held a PhD, and they weren't worthy to hold Benjamin's coat.

"I was just going to say," he said, perhaps thinking I knew what he was trying to say, "the stone that makes this house outstanding was in the ground in Winnsboro. From a hole in the ground it breeds beauty."

"It cannot be judged by how far it has come from what it was," I said, "but where it is now."

"People seldom judge right," Benjamin added. "Let the voice inside be the judge."

"No one could have said it better," I answered.

Chapter Twenty-two

I picked Mother up at the bus station in Charleston and we headed to Myrtle Beach, where we planned to celebrate Christmas with Jonny. Jonny had moved into an apartment on Thirty-first Avenue North, a block and a half inland from the ocean and only a few steps to the school where she worked. The houses in that block were neat, mostly owned by families who had lived in Myrtle Beach for years. Mr. and Mrs. Ward had built a smaller house in back of their home, planning to use it for their grandchildren when they came to visit. The "grands" rarely came, and the Wards rented the small stucco house to Jonny.

The house that we called "Jonny's house" was painted yellow. It was neat and clean and close to everything we wanted to do during the holidays. A doughnut shop was on the Kings Highway, within a block, and we ate breakfast there. We snacked during the day and splurged at night, dining at the Sea Captain's House, on the ocean and about one and a half blocks away. A time or two we really splurged and dined at the Ocean Forest Hotel, a mile or two north, off the Kings Highway and facing the ocean.

A wedding reception was in progress when we entered the Ocean Forest Hotel on December 23. The night was warm and balmy and many of the members of the wedding party were on the terrace. They were having a grand time, and I wondered if I could have such a wedding and reception.

The maître d-hôtel seated us near a window, where we could see the ocean. We were in the southernmost part of the room and the bridal party took up most of the rest of the large room. I eyed the bride and groom. They didn't stay together as I would have believed, but she went from table to table, talking to her friends, some of them probably former roommates, and he was obviously joking around with his buddies. An organist played "White Christmas," "Here Comes Santa Claus" and "Silent Night." I was swamped with the magic of the evening and pictured myself and Benjamin. But then again, I still wasn't absolutely sure everything would happen as planned.

"You know," I said to Jonny and Mother, "I love Benjamin. He can give me everything a girl ever dreamed of, but I don't have that feeling of ecstasy one should have before marriage. Where is it? What's wrong with me?"

"I don't know what's wrong with you," Jonny quipped, "but while you're making up your mind, Benjamin Bodicott is going to be tapped by another woman. When you don't have the option to marry him, you'll wish you had found that ecstasy."

Mother nodded her head. "I think, Whaley, that you'll be making a horrible mistake if you let him slip through your fingers."

"If I were in your place, I'd grab him and take off for the nearest justice of the peace," Jonny said. "A rich, single man gets shot down real fast."

I realized I would have to come to an absolute, unequivocal conclusion. And soon.

"Leap to it, and don't wait," Jonny urged.

We dined on roast beef and ended our meal with a slice of Mrs. Roosevelt's lemon cheesecake, then rode slowly down the Kings Highway to Jonny's abode. It was a starry night, the kind one hopes for when in Myrtle Beach. Jonny's little house had a bedroom and small bath upstairs, which she claimed as hers. Mother and I slept in two bedrooms downstairs. We went to bed early. With the breakers roaring in my ears, I thought about all that had been said about my impending marriage.

The next morning we went shopping at Chapins. Last-minute Christmas shoppers were everywhere. Jonny picked up several boxes of chocolate-covered cherries. The weather had turned cooler and we welcomed it. Christmas called for cold weather. Driving back to Thirty-first Avenue North, we passed the Sea Captain's House and decided we would eat there that evening.

Huge wreaths hung on the big wooden door. When we stepped inside, the scent of a wood-burning fireplace met us. The woman at the counter took our names and asked us to wait until my name was called. She pointed us in the direction of a large bowl of hot wassail. We ambled over and Jonny ladled steaming apple cider into cups and handed them to Mother and me. We found seats near the fire. I didn't think I had ever had been so cozy on a Christmas Eve. The sofas were big and soft and notes of "Ave Maria" drifted from an organ someone was playing. When I sipped the last of the hot, spicy cider, I held onto my cup. I hadn't had nearly enough of that. I was standing at the wassail bowl when a waiter motioned for us to come to the porch. I quickly filled my cup and we followed him. I told him the glass-enclosed porch with its wonderful view of the ocean was our first choice of where to be on Christmas Eve.

We settled in at a table by a window facing the ocean. Mother and I sat on one side of the table and Johnny on the other. We gazed at the scene beyond the window. The sun was going down.

Bright lights from the roof of the building shined on the ocean, where there appeared to be hundreds of gulls flying, soaring and alighting in the surf. We didn't say a word until our rapture with the gulls was interrupted by a waitress, awaiting our orders. All three of us ordered select oysters. A basket of hush puppies was brought to our table. We slathered them in butter, gobbled them down and waited for the entrées to arrive. Jonny took our cups back to the wassail bowl and refilled them.

Our meal started with a salad, fresh and delicious. We enjoyed it without talking. Each entrée arrived on a large platter. A mound of oysters was surrounded by green beans, broccoli and carrots, cooked lightly and seasoned with mild spices. I asked for a refill on the basket of hush puppies. Jonny and I ordered iced tea and Mother asked for a cup of coffee.

"Isn't this wonderful?" Mother asked, looking toward the horizon. "I don't know what I would do without my two girls." Jonny looked at me questioningly. Mother rarely became sentimental. Her words warmed my heart and Jonny had tears in her eyes. "I hope we have many years to enjoy other occasions such as this one," Mother said.

"We will," Jonny promised.

"I would like to come here, to Myrtle Beach, more often," Mother said. "I've always liked Myrtle Beach."

"I don't see why you can't visit often," Jonny said. "I like it here. The people are cordial. My work is satisfying. I don't plan on leaving anytime soon."

Mother reached across the table for Jonny's hand and placed her other hand on mine, which was resting on the table. "I've something to tell you," she said.

Jonny's eyes circled around to mine. We were in awe. What was

Mother about to reveal to us? I wondered.

"I love both of you with my heart," she began. "Times change. Nothing stays the same for very long."

"It surely doesn't," Jonny added.

"I like living close to Cousin Mag and Cousin Shirley." Mother went on, letting go of our hands and turning to look at us. "You don't know them, really, not as I do, having been raised close to my cousins and seeing them frequently during my early years. We talk about the old folks, most of them lying in the cemetery now, and it gets right funny sometimes. I had forgotten, totally forgotten, about some of the people I really liked back then."

"Get to the point, Mother," Jonny said, appearing to expect the worst.

"If I'm going to stay in Jacksonville, and it would be an insult to leave them now, I've got to think of the future. I didn't think in those terms until I received the letter."

"What letter?" I queried.

"The letter from Mr. Devine."

"You mean the real estate man?" Jonny asked pointedly.

"Yes," Mother replied. "He made me a right good offer for the farm."

"You mean the house I live in?" I asked.

Mother put her hand on my knee and gave a little squeeze. "Yes. It's an old house, but the land is worth a good bit."

"I'd like to know what you call a 'good bit,'" Jonny said. She seemed to be getting a little edgy.

"I would as well," I said. "I live there."

Mother ignored our requests. "Whaley, you're getting married. You're going to live in a mansion. What would you want with that old house?"

"I'm not married yet," I spat. "Who knows? I plan on marrying Benjamin but we haven't said "til death do us part.""

Mother braced her shoulders. I pushed my plate back, unable to take another bite. Jonny took her fork and moved the oysters around on her plate. "I'm going to accept Mr. Devine's offer," Mother said. "I don't need to worry about that property any longer." She looked at me. "Whaley, you will not be thrown out on the street, as your eyes tell me you are thinking."

I didn't know what to say and quietly looked at Mother.

"It's not like I'm selling the house tomorrow," Mother explained. "These transactions take time." Neither Jonny nor I was interested in anything else she had to say. It was hard to imagine the house where we grew up belonging to someone else. We couldn't help but feel angry and a bit betrayed. She changed the subject, but Jonny and I didn't take the bait. We sat in silence for a few minutes and just looked around the room. It had taken on a chilly mode. The waitress came and I believed she was a little bossy. I asked for our check.

I paid the bill at the door and we walked a few blocks on Ocean Boulevard. I noticed a little girl and two dogs on the other side of the street. I crossed over and Mother and Jonny came behind me. "Tell me about your dogs," I said to the little girl.

"They're for sale," she said. "This one is four dollars and the one with brown spots is six dollars because he's a boy."

I patted both dogs. The male dog wagged his tail. I couldn't push my bitterness aside. "If I had a home I would buy the boy," I said. Turning back and staring at the Sea Captain's House, I added, "I would name him Hush Puppy."

We went back to the car and drove to the southern end of Ocean Boulevard and back again, entering the Dunes Club on the northern end of the city and looking at the grand homes facing the sea. A few minutes before midnight we entered the sanctuary of the First Methodist Church, on the corner of Kings Highway and Ninth Avenue. "Silent Night" was coming from the pipes of the organ. We found seats on a pew near the chancel. Just then a star in the eaves of the church took fire. More lights appeared, stroking the carved faces of a Nativity scene on a table at the altar. I looked around at the families seated near us. Their devotion for one another seemed to have been reinforced from the tender scene of the crèche. It was a sublime moment as the faces of the people gathered in the church radiated the glow of the holy family. How was it that I could have discordant feelings for my mother on such a night as this, I wondered.

On Christmas morning we exchanged gifts. Mother gave Jonny and me red flannel robes. "To keep you warm and comfy," she explained. I gave her a dressing gown. The blouse portion was of black velvet, the skirt of red and green taffeta. "To keep you stylish and snazzy around your relatives," I said. Jonny gave her a candle in a silver holder. "To throw some warm light on the long, boring nights you spend with Uncle Fletch," she commented.

Jonny and I helped Mother gather her things and get ready to go. "We can't tarry," I urged. "The bus for Savannah leaves at three o'clock."

On the way to Charleston, Mother again tried to rationalize the sale of the farm. "Tax time is coming up," she said. "Paying insurance on the house will follow. The expenses are more than I can handle. I don't want the burden of planting cotton next year.

That was your Daddy's job. You'll be getting married soon and you and Benjamin will start a new life. And Jonny has a good life in Myrtle Beach."

I began to see she was right. Why should she hold onto a farm with an old house and the worries it would bring? It was right for her to sell it and Jonny and I could look out for ourselves. Perhaps I could ask Hannah if she would help me find a place to live for a while in Charleston. Benjamin's house was nearly completed, but I wanted more time to think things through. Suddenly I was filled with the desire to live in Charleston. If anything was available for me in Charleston, Hannah would know about it.

Mother and I went into the bus station and took a seat while we awaited the arrival of the bus she would take to Jacksonville. "I'm thinking about taking an apartment in Charleston," I said, "while you sort out the farm. I'll talk it over with my friend, Hannah Vanderhorst."

Mother's face took on a curious expression. "You still plan to marry Benjamin, do you not?"

"Well, I think so. But I need some time to think that over. Besides, his house isn't quite ready and I just think I would enjoy living in Charleston for a while." The Savannah departure was announced. We got up and I carried Mother's bag to the bus and got her settled in a seat near the front. I kissed her good-bye and left.

When I got home, a narrow, long, beautifully wrapped Christmas gift lay at the door. I carried it into my bedroom and opened it. Sparkling in the beam of the overhead light was a long-stemmed, tapered rosebud. It appeared to be of the finest crystal on which my eyes had ever rested. A Christmas card was enclosed, signed in Daddy's script, *Benjamin Bodicott*. My tears did nothing to drown the tenderness I felt for Benjamin, writing one of the two scripts he could write, his name and the name of his business. His name was perfectly written in the script Daddy had jotted down on the paper at the Feed and Seed long ago. "Oh *Benjamin. Daddy,*" I cried as I made my way to the Baldwin grand and played "Maria Elena."

Before I went to bed, I put the crystal rosebud in a vase and placed it on the piano.

Chapter Twenty-three

On Monday, Hannah and I walked to the hole-in-the-wall restaurant for lunch. I told her my mother had been made an offer on the farm, and that meant I would need a place to live for a while. I went on to say that it would be likely I would get married before too long and wouldn't need to stay forever. She didn't elaborate on my move to Charleston, but brought up the subject of Benjamin's house.

"It's beautiful," I said. "I don't mean to brag but it is beautiful, mostly of Winnsboro blue granite, and some bricks around the entrance. The patio faces the marsh and I think that will be a favorite place to spend time, but there is a sunroom on the inland exposure with three walls of glass. It *is* stunning, especially when you're driving toward the house and the sunroom is flooded with the sun. As you leave the Edisto Road and turn in to the property, that room is visible all the way through the fields and until you arrive at the house."

"You're just lucky," Hannah said. "You've had a streak of luck or you're very blessed to find a fine man who is a nice fellow and rich to boot. Everyone loves Edisto Island. Even the people who live in the Charleston mansions covet those who live on the island."

"Yeah, well, it's relative," I mused.

"What do you mean?" Hannah asked.

"Like Benjamin said, 'We all want something the other fellow has.' He also said that the wonderful blue granite stone was only rocks in the ground until it was fashioned into a house."

Chapter Twenty-four

Two days later Hannah and I were again on our way to the hole-in-the-wall restaurant when she said, "Oh by the way, Mother, Julia and I talked over your situation. Mother brought up the subject that our house has a third floor that's rarely used. Actually, the bedroom up there is the nicest in the house because it has an adjoining bathroom. We've never rented it and Mother never intends to. She said you could stay there as long as you want, providing you do not expect meals, housecleaning services and things like that. She said you're a friend and she wouldn't feel right about charging you a penny. She says all of us would be better off with you in the house."

I stopped in my tracks. "*Really?*"

"Word for word. We would like for somebody to be up there, someone we know."

"Not a ghost," I quipped.

Hannah laughed. "There are stories of a ghost on the stairway—we *have* heard steps on the stairway at night. But it's only folklore. Still, we would like for you to take the room if you think you can put up with us."

"I *am* very blessed. This particular blessing has come at a time when I need a break. I lost my Daddy and now our house. I had begun to wonder when my bad luck would end."

"The room is ready when you are."

"I'll let you know tomorrow," I said. "I'd like to move in sooner rather than later."

"That's just fine by us," Hannah said.

I stopped by the Feed and Seed on my way home that night. Benjamin was at the counter, glancing at the pictures in a catalog. I ran around the counter, grabbed him and kissed him on the lips. "Thank you for the gorgeous crystal rosebud," I whispered, my lips still touching his. "It was my favorite Christmas present."

He gave me a little squeeze and said, "I'm glad you like it. Give me a minute to close the store and we'll sit on the porch."

Sitting on a porch in rockers is such an *Edisto* thing, I was thinking as I sat down. Everybody, even in the South Carolina Lowcountry, didn't have the option of sitting on a porch during December. "My luck changed today," I said casually.

"Oh?" A quizzical look spread across his face.

"Actually, you didn't know it, but my luck faded during the last few days. Mother is selling the farm."

"Your mother is selling the farm?"

"Yep. When she first told us, Jonny and I nearly fainted. And to tell you the truth, I don't think I have ever been so angry in my entire life. Then Mother mentioned the taxes, insurance and how the fields had to be planted, and I knew she could never take care of the place. It's the right thing to do, but it's not easy. The only thing that came easily is the room my friends will let me use for a while—my friend who works in the tax office, Hannah Vanderhorst, has invited me to stay in a third-floor bedroom of their family home on Tradd Street in Charleston."

"You're going to *live* there?"

"Well, yes. That is, I'll live there until I move in with you. *Our* house is not ready to be occupied, and I need a place to stay until that time. Talk about luck, with the way Mother's luck has been going lately she'll sell the house tomorrow. I'm fortunate to have a friend who would make me such a generous offer. Mr. Devine has the contract on the farm and as you well know, his properties move fast."

"I know also that our house will be ready for us to move in by the first of May."

"Benjamin! Really? In five months? I didn't expect it to be ready quite so soon."

He paused and I could almost see his mind tossing like the ever-rolling waves. If what he had told me was true, and I had no reason ever to doubt Benjamin, he had lived a life in the manner of the homeless sea gulls I had viewed from the Sea Captain's House in Myrtle Beach. At nightfall they tucked in their wings and were rocked to sleep in the cold, surging billows. It wasn't much of a home. Certainly not one of the kind he so deeply desired.

"I'm thinking," he said, "if we could be married about the middle of April, and go on a honeymoon trip to The Cloister Hotel at Sea Island, Georgia, we could be home sometime around the first of May."

"But springtime is your busiest season in the store. Who'll sell the fertilizer and seeds?"

"I've hired a staff."

"Staff?" I was aghast. Honeymooning at The Cloister at Sea Island sounded wonderful, just beyond any honeymoon I could have dreamed up, but where had he found a staff?

"You remember George Gaud?"

"Where do you think I've been all these years? He's a son of the caretaker of one of the Hutton plantations."

"He wants to work for me. He'll be ready to take over by the first of March."

I couldn't take all of it in. It was just too much. A few hours ago I had agreed to move into the Vanderhorst house on Tradd Street and now we were talking a honeymoon at The Cloister at Sea Island and moving into the stone mansion on the ridge. Things were moving too fast. I was dizzy with plans being made, plans over which I seemed to have no control.

Benjamin must have recognized my confusion. He got up, took a few steps and stopped. "We'll thrash all of this out in a day or so. I'm going home with you and see that you're safe there. You need to get some rest."

"Okay, but I'm going to move all my clothes to the car tonight. I'll sleep at the farm tonight and move my things to the Vanderhorst house tomorrow. It's likely I won't be back in Edisto until Tuesday when I'll get my books and take a music lesson."

Benjamin seemed down and out. "I'll follow you home," he said.

I got in the red Dodge, Benjamin in his truck, and we headed for the house. Everything Benjamin said sounded good, but I didn't take time to digest his plans. I was thinking of packing—I didn't have a lot of clothes to be moved, just a few wool suits and some shoes.

We walked up the front steps side-by-side. I took a suitcase from the closet and threw it on the bed. Benjamin was watching me. In seconds, it seemed, my underclothes and pajamas were packed.

"I wish you were packing for our honeymoon at The Cloister," he said dreamily.

"Me, too."

"Here. Let me help you with that," he said, reaching for a bag. He carried it out and put it in my car. I took some clothes on hangers from the closet and lay them on the bed. My suits were not designer clothes but I took care of them. Plastic bags covered the wool skirts and jackets. Benjamin came in and got a load for the car. It wasn't long before we were almost finished. As he lifted the last of the clothes on hangers, he said, "I would like it if you would play a piece for me. On the piano."

"Okay. What would you like? Not that I can take requests. But I know a couple."

"What's your favorite?" he asked.

"'Maria Elena.'" I didn't explain that Daddy had a passion for that piece.

"Play that."

I waited until Benjamin took the rest of my clothes to the car. He came back to the living room and sat in what we called an "easy chair" and lifted his feet to the ottoman. I played the haunting song. He tilted his head back, closed his eyes and said, "Play it again." It was clear he was enjoying the music.

I had come to the place where I could play "Maria Elena" without looking at the notes and lately I had been adding a few chords of my own. By jazzing it up a little I felt I was becoming more of an expert at playing it.

I slid around on the bench and looked at Benjamin, really looked at him. He was at home here. My family was his family. They liked him. As they said, *he was a good man*. He had virtues hidden in his soul, goodness that I didn't know about. Invisible morality lurked there. His soul was like the rich stone in the bowels of the earth, stones that lacked the luminescence of a ruby or the brilliance of a diamond, but stones that were well-fitting, made to endure, worth living with.

When Benjamin was gone I called Mother and told her I was moving to Charleston the next day. She asked me when I would be back in the house on Edisto and I told her I would come back next

155

Tuesday to take a music lesson. I dropped the phone in the cradle, wondering why she wanted to know when I would be back. What difference did it make? Actually none, except she probably just wanted to be sure someone was keeping an eye on the place.

Chapter Twenty-five

*H*annah, Julia and I were sisters under our skins. We three sprawled on the high bed in the third-story bedroom and talked until the deep night crept upon us. Julia couldn't get enough talk of Benjamin. "You'll marry him soon, I know it," she said.

"Who wouldn't?" asked Hannah.

"Maybe I won't," I put in, though I wasn't sure I believed myself anymore. I loved him.

"You will," Julia insisted. "I'm not a soothsayer but I know it. A man like that doesn't come along every day."

"Benjamin takes pride in himself," I blurted out. "He wears nice clothes and walks as though he's parading down Pennsylvania Avenue. But he's not perfect."

"What's not perfect?" Hannah asked.

"No one is perfect. *I'm* not. If I knew the truth about Judge Parker even he probably is not perfect."

"Okay. I take your word for it. But to me, Benjamin Bodicott is about as perfect as a man can be," Hannah said.

"By the way, on Tuesday I'm going back to Edisto for a music lesson. I'll be back here that night, but not real early. Sometimes Charlotte Ann keeps me longer than usual. In other words, don't look for me until you see me."

"Will you see Benjamin on Tuesday?" Julia wanted to know.

"Maybe. Maybe not. He knows I'm coming home to take the lesson."

"If you ever get to the place where you don't want him, let me know," Hannah said.

"And I'm second in line," Julia added.

Chapter Twenty-six

$\mathcal{D}$riving toward home, I passed the Feed and Seed. Benjamin saw me pass and waved. I was running late and didn't stop, but he must have left quickly because he wasn't far behind when I pulled the red Dodge into the yard.

"You going for a music lesson?" he called as I got out of my car.

"That I am. Want to go with me?"

"Yes. I like to walk the grounds."

"I'd enjoy your company," I said.

He got out of the truck, kissed me on the forehead and we flew up the steps to the porch. He backed me against the door. "Have you thought about the honeymoon? What do you think?"

I was thinking how much Hannah and Julia wished they were in my place at that moment, but I answered, "It sounds wonderful, Benjamin."

"I think you'll like The Cloister."

"Have you ever been there?" I asked.

"A time or two. We had some meetings there when we were involved in selling the island."

I unlocked the door and we walked inside. Benjamin was behind me. The house was empty. Not a stick of furniture was in the living room. Not a curtain, not a window shade. I felt a cry rush through my throat and lips as I dashed to the vacant space where the piano had been. There was no piano.

"Someone came like a thief in the night and took away everything, including my piano," I cried.

Benjamin tried to comfort me. "Calm down. We don't know what the circumstances are. The piano is somewhere and we'll find it. I promise you."

Suddenly I knew what had happened. I just *knew*. "Benjamin! My mother has sold the farm and taken the furniture to Jacksonville, including my piano. She didn't know that Daddy told me it was *mine*. He never got a chance…"

"Calm down," Benjamin said. "You'll make yourself sick."

"My mother came, took my piano and without a word she left me to grieve for it."

Benjamin was thinking back. "We were here five days ago. Since that time the house has been emptied." He took my arm to lead me out.

"No. I'm not ready to go yet. I want to see all of it, every vacant room."

We walked slowly down the hall, glancing into each room. An old skirt and a sweater I had not taken to Charleston hung in the closet of the back bedroom. That was it. Everything else was gone. We walked back toward the living room. "I have no music book. I can't go to Charlotte Ann's and tell her about this. I would blubber all over her. But then again, I have to go there and tell her that I will not be back. My music career has come to an end." I turned to Benjamin and slung my head against his chest. *Give me your peace*, I was thinking. *Where is it?* Then it came flooding into me and I began to sob, wild, loud, gasping sobs.

"Let's go to The Claw and have a cup of coffee," Benjamin suggested. "Your face is drained."

We left the red Dodge parked in the yard and went to the small restaurant in Benjamin's truck. Dreadfully nervous, I slid into a booth and ordered black coffee. I started talking as though I were wound up. "Legally, everything in the house belongs to my mother. My old skirt and sweater were in the closet where I always kept them. The solution to the mystery is obvious: Mother took what she believed was hers and left my possessions here. That clue gives us a perfect understanding of her reasoning. Her motive, if she had one, was to take everything to Jacksonville and distribute it among her cousins and their families. Thinking back, I believe I heard someone say that Cousin Mag's grandson has bought a house and has no furniture to put in it. Now he has a Baldwin grand among his household goods!

"The big decision for me is this: *How does one consider a missing piano without a mountain of embarrassment?* An embarrassment of family, that's what it is. Be that as it may, I refuse to show remorse for anything Mother did, especially taking the piano away." I glanced at Benjamin. His mouth was slightly ajar, trying to take in all I was saying. "Remember that on this day I said I would have *no* remorse. I won't. But…with all reason against it…my mind is telling me to have some compassion for her. Mother must have had her own purpose for taking the piano, if not for the reason of having two daughters and one piano then perhaps for the reason of some debt she envisions she owes her cousins. If I were to face her now, right this very minute, she would have some sort of an excuse that would seem reasonable. She worked hard for us. She made our clothes, scrubbed them on the washboard until she was endowed forever with reddened hands and cooked biscuits from scratch three times a day every day of her of life.

"When I have the time to sit and analyze the situation, I'll probably come to the conclusion that the missing piano was more a fault with Daddy than Mother. He told me many times that he didn't know how he would handle it but the piano was mine. I took him at his word. Mother and Jonny knew nothing of Daddy's plans for the piano. He could have called all of us together, said he wanted me to have the piano and given Jonny a sum of money for her part of the instrument. She would rather have money any day than a piano. Why could he not just face Mother and explain how he wanted it handled? We'll never know. And it's done. Sulking over it will help none of us. I will not, now or ever, discuss the matter with Jonny. There is no question she would regard Mother's reasoning as honest and fair.

"Benjamin, this is what it has come down to."

"Tell me."

"We will leave here and go to Charlotte Ann's house, where I will cancel all music lessons. I'll use as an excuse the fact that I have moved to Charleston. In the near future, I expect all of the islanders to render skillful queries about the piano and the furniture, but their inquiries will elicit no sympathy or consideration from me. Oh yes, a sensation would run sweet in some of their veins, but it would turn my heart to marble. Better the piano and furniture be left alone. I will maintain a profound silence of the subject to everyone other than you. "

"What you have modified in respect to the exactitude, with reluctance to terms of probability, and comparing the deductions of the premises and notoriety, nothing is more applicable to individual impressions."

Though I suspected Benjamin did not understand all of what he had uttered, I could tell he realized this was a matter that demanded the greatest secrecy. *What would I do without him?*

We got in the truck and left.

Chapter Twenty-seven

*S*tanding at Charlotte Ann's door, I felt my teeth clinch but tried to repress the current of my mind's rage. My goal to learn to play the piano would not be fulfilled, but I would give all of it up rather than cause a sensation that would embarrass my mother beyond all telling. I loved my mother.

"Hey Whaley, come in," Charlotte Ann called.

"I can't come in this time."

"But you have a music lesson."

"There's something I want to tell you, Charlotte Ann. It's not the easiest thing to explain, but I'll try. The afternoons, after a day of tedious work at the courthouse, are so short. Some Charleston friends suggested I move into an unused room in their house. I like the arrangement and enjoy living in Charleston, but I won't be taking lessons for a while."

Something was happening all around me. Could it be a silent funeral? I tried to discern who had died but there was no body to bury. Then, like a flick of darkness, it was gone. A time to remember. A time of parting. A time for good-bye.

"I'm sorry to hear that," Charlotte was saying. "You were getting along so well. You're my star student. I tell everybody that. Will you still be playing in the recital this spring?"

"Don't count on me," I answered. "Things are piling up on my calendar. I'll come back and talk to you later."

"I'll look forward to your visit, Whaley. You're progressing with your music and it would be disastrous if you abandoned your work.

I've noticed some real progress just lately. I'll make a few notes and have some things in mind for you when you return."

"Thank you, Charlotte Ann. Just as you could not possibly count all of the pieces you have taught your students to play, I cannot find the ways to tell you how much I enjoyed your lessons. You're an excellent teacher. I'll…be back."

I got in the truck and rested my head in my hands. Something, or could it have been someone, had left my life. I felt it all around me.

"Whaley?" Benjamin said. "Whaley, I just remembered something. A lady came into the store this week and left a letter for you."

"Who was it?"

"I don't know. I never saw her, or perhaps I did see her, once, at your house, when Mr. DeShazo played the piano."

"Oh, please. Don't talk about that night. I want to forget that night as long as I live. I'll play it in my head like an old movie and hear the sounds, smell the scents, remember the people and see the piano in my mind's eye. Who was the lady?"

"I don't know. She said she didn't have your Charleston address and left the letter for me to hand to you."

"Let's go back and get it, and then I have to go back to Charleston. The Vanderhorsts will run me away if I start getting home late."

We went into the store and Benjamin took a letter from the moneybox.

The return address read: *Callie Middleton Wilde.*

"What does she want from me?"

"She didn't say," Benjamin answered.

"She was rather cool to me during school days but really buttered Mother up after Daddy's death." I tore open the letter.

Dear Whaley,
We, the Class of 1951, are having a Reunion to be held at the Church of the Tides Leisure Ministries Building on February 9. We all look forward to seeing you. A social hour begins at 4:00 p.m. and dinner will start at 5:00 p.m. The meal is being catered by the Lodge members and will include salad, steak and vegetables, and Mrs. Jenkins's coconut cake. The cost is $4.00 per person. If you send in your payment and should be unable to attend, the $4.00 will be refunded. You can come as a single or bring a friend. We look forward to seeing you there.
Callie.

I was inclined to throw the invitation away. I wouldn't go to the reunion for all the world's riches. Or would I?

"What's that all about?" Benjamin asked.

With a flourish, I lifted my arm and dropped the note on the counter. "The class of 1951 is having a reunion on February 9. Perish the thought of the torment of having to spend an evening with that crowd."

"You're not going?"

"Yes, of course I'm going. I'm not about to withdraw from the island society and start a sensation of my own. I expect to fully face up to the members of the class of 1951."

Benjamin came over and took me in his arms. I put my head in that special place on his chest. "Will you come here to the Feed and Seed on this Saturday evening? I'll have a secret item to show you."

"What is it?"

"If I told you it would not be a secret."

"Thank you, Benjamin, for being my rock during these difficult times."

"That's my job. You're my woman."

"See you on Saturday."

Chapter Twenty-eight

I started the day on Saturday by cleaning my room. As I swept the hardwood floors and changed the linen on the bed, I was considering what I believed could be the beginning of a glittering Charleston social life, short-lived though it would be, and I was conscious of a little upper-class smile developing. I wasn't a blue blood and never aspired to become a member of Charleston society, but Julia and Hannah and their mother had introduced me to some of the aristocracy. They were quite nice, really, and they accepted the little learned smile as genteel. I didn't intend to give in to it, but I couldn't say life hadn't dared to send a challenge to indulge in some of Charleston's polished principles behind the pillars of the homes. I believed I could handle it. On the other hand, the Charlestonians clung together in their affluent society and one had to work at attaining membership. I liked island life, although it had its drawbacks. An English poet once said that no man is an island, entire of itself. I sat on the bed to think about that for a minute. No one *is* an island, I thought, but when one lived *on* an island, it was as though it were entire of itself. If a light went on at four o'clock in the morning, someone came to see if something had happened. Had the woman of the house gone into labor? Was someone sick? Should a physician be summoned? When worst came to worst, the island people cleaned the house, cooked food and took care of their own. Many of them were rich but unfamiliar with wealth. Others lived in luxury. Some, having made their fortunes in the North, came south to attain that symbol of wealth, a Southern plantation.

As a friend of the Vanderhorst family, it was likely I would be invited to the cream of Charleston society's parties. It might be that I would find Charleston society boring, but then again, to live in Charleston and be out of it would be a tragedy.

"Wanna do lunch at McCrady's?" Julia called from downstairs.

McCrady's was a delightful restaurant on East Bay. Unlike the Sea Captain's House in Myrtle Beach, one could not dine and look at the sea, but McCrady's had its own special atmosphere. "Be down in a minute," I called. I didn't tell Julia that Benjamin had something to tell me and she had no idea that I was going to drive to Edisto later in the day. I decided not to divulge that little tidbit. The most important little mystery was one I would keep locked inside forever. As I dwelled on it, it became clear I was hoarding something I couldn't even name. My mother had disposed of my Baldwin grand. Somewhere the piano stood at that moment. Someone might even be playing it. I would never know where it was and I would never ask. Even though I was not a Charlestonian some of their edicts were correct: whatever I did I must hold up appearances. I would not be an ostrich with my head in the sand, but I would stand studiously neutral. There would be no grouping of rivalries, but a structure of common peace.

We were seated at a booth at McCreary's. We ordered she crab soup. "I wonder if this was made with orange eggs," Julia said.

"What in the world are you talking about? It looks a little pink," I replied.

"She crab soup was perfected at the John Rutledge House, on Broad Street," Julia explained. "One evening a long time ago, after the soup cook had finished the crab bouillabaisse for a ball, another cook said it looked bland. The soup cook took it back to the kitchen. The carcasses of the crabs lay on a table. The cook noticed some orange-reddish eggs attached to some of the shells. A light went on in her head and she added the orange egg yolks to the soup. Like magic, the eggs turned the bouillabaisse pink, anything but bland. The eggs, of course, came from the female crabs, 'she crabs' the cooks called them in their Gullah language. The origin of she crab soup is your Charleston lesson for today."

"It's delicious, orange eggs or not," I said.

We ended the meal with a dessert of meringue and coffee. I realized that I was more relaxed than I had been in days. I couldn't remember when I had such peace within myself. During the last days I had known little but imagined everything. It had taken its toll. Julia and I talked about Charleston and her upbringing. She told me about some of the wonderful houses and who owned them.

"Which is your favorite?" I asked.

"No person could choose one Charleston house over the others," she explained. "Each one has it specialties. It's said in England that a living room is not a proper living room without a grand piano and a bit of safari."

"Safari?"

"It goes back to the days when England owned Africa. The English always displayed a pillow or a tapestry or something featuring a tiger or lion. Each drawing room had its grand piano, unless the house had a music room, and of course the piano was in the music room if there was one."

"How interesting," I said as I continued to think about the decorating features, trying to keep my mind *off* the piano. "But that has never been true in Charleston, has it?"

"Not to a high degree, although a lot of the drawing rooms have a grand piano and there usually is a touch of safari."

"That's nice," I said, looking at my watch. "I've got to go. Benjamin is expecting me at Edisto this afternoon. I'll be home early."

"Will you and Benjamin be discussing any upcoming events?" Julia asked, a twinkle in her eye.

"None that I know of."

We walked toward the Vanderhorst home. It was a lovely stroll. Wisteria was vining and birds were nesting. When we arrived at Julia's home she ducked under a limb of a magnolia tree and darted to the porch. She turned and waved. I tooted the horn and was on my way to Edisto Island.

Chapter Twenty-nine

I was looking at my watch when I pulled the red Dodge into the parking area of the Feed and Seed. Benjamin stood in the doorway. He was smiling brightly and I thought, for the zillionth time, that he really had a good mouth and nice teeth. He met me at the car. "I'll close up in about thirty minutes and we'll have time for a nice meal before you see the surprise."

"I'm impatient as the wind when it comes to surprises," I said. "What is it, Benjamin? I can't wait."

"You must wait. I'll give it to you in the dark."

"The dark? I can't imagine what it is. Is it rarer than gold?"

"For you? Absolutely. For others? No."

"It's a ring, an engagement ring."

Benjamin's expression had the glitter of a diamond, something I had not discerned earlier. I got out of the car and held him close, turning my face away from him. I hadn't expected an engagement ring and if I let him slip it on my finger I would be committed to go through with all of his plans for our wedding and honeymoon at The Cloister. I loved the very idea of all he was offering, but was I truly ready to make the commitment? I wondered. If I went along, it would be forever and eternity where I was concerned. Divorce was absurd to me. I couldn't conceive of any circumstances that would allow divorce. If one knew the person of choice, then nothing that person would or would not do could render the means for a divorce. How well did I know Benjamin? I thought I knew him very well, including his secret.

He kissed me on the forehead and went to lock up. Coming back to me, he twirled his car keys on a finger. "Got a date with a dream girl," he cooed. He was different somehow. Almost frivolous. I liked him this way.

Benjamin drove to Beaufort, where he had made reservations at a waterfront restaurant. He ordered wine. Members of a band tuned their instruments and the notes led into "Up a Lazy River." Benjamin got up and asked me to dance.

"I can't dance," I said, thinking back to high school when the jitterbug was all the rage.

He turned me a couple of times and I naturally swung back into his arms. "Could have fooled me," he said. Dancing with him was the most natural thing. I *couldn't* dance. I had never thought of taking dancing lessons and always believed that nature had structured a sort of geometrical coordination system that never made its way into my body. It had something to do with triangles, rectangles, circles and poetry, and on the day when dancing was passed out I was not there. On this occasion, for some reason I couldn't fathom, I felt light on my feet and they were keeping the rhythm. When the band stopped playing, Benjamin took me to my seat.

"I really enjoyed that," I said.

"You sound surprised."

"I am. I haven't danced in years. I haven't *ever* danced."

"You have danced. You shall dance on our patio in the moonlight."

"Oh, Benjamin. That sounds perfect."

"It will be wonderful. Let's order. Not only am I hungry, but I also have a gift to deliver."

My ring, I was thinking. I wondered what it would look like. Was it yellow gold or platinum? Was it a solitaire or did baguettes surround the predominant stone? What would I say? What if I couldn't think of just the right thing to say and made a commitment I could not live up to? If Benjamin placed the ring on my finger, it would be forever. I would not remove it. I would go to the end, finish the race. If that wasn't possible for me, the ring would not go on my finger. For once in my life I had to know what to do and I had to do the right thing.

"Beef or salmon?" he asked.

"Filet mignon," I answered.

"Same for me," Benjamin put in.

We were served a salad, and while we ate, a huge yacht drifted by.

"Is that Mrs. Hutton's vessel?" Benjamin asked.

"No. Her yacht has sails. She's a beaut. So white and sleek." I watched the ship go out of sight and we continued eating. "It's getting dark," I said.

Our salad plates were taken away and the steak put before us. We talked very little as we ate. The meat was tender and juicy, and I enjoyed a hot yeast roll with it. Finally we were finished and Benjamin ordered chocolate cake for dessert. I passed on that.

"It's awfully dark," I said again as we motored on Highway 17, back to Edisto.

"Just right."

"Just right for what?" I queried.

"For the presentation of a gift."

I began to think that the time was near. No more time to reflect. It was going to be now or never. I couldn't make a mistake. I cleared my throat and shook my head. A clear head was a necessity. My grandchildren would hear reminiscences of this night. What I do or do not do must be accurate, according to the laws of all that's holy, I thought. I cannot mess this up, I told myself. I pictured my father and all of my family, including my grandparents. Every one of them had gone into marriage knowing it was the right thing to do, ready for whatever unfolded. They lived good, upright lives. Not a smear was on their record.

Benjamin was turning into the long drive that led to the new house. He drove slowly, saying very little. My mind was in turmoil.

"I believe a light is on. Is a light on in the house?" I asked.

"Yes, a light is on, and I have a confession to make."

"What is it?"

"I have lied to you."

I put my hands over my face. I thought he was going to tell me about his past. I tried to keep my voice even. "What did you lie about?"

"I told you the room with the glass walls was a sunroom. It was never intended to be a sunroom."

I was now quite confused. The sunroom? "What is it?" I asked.

"It's a music room."

"But Benjamin—you know about my piano. What will we do with a music room?"

He just grinned at me and continued driving down the lane. It was now plain to see that a large piece of furniture was in the room.

"Something's *in* the room."

Benjamin pulled the car nearer.

"Benjamin, it's a piano." I felt my heart racing in my chest.

"A Baldwin grand, your wedding gift from me," he said.

I was speechless. I looked at him and felt my eyes watering. "Benjamin. You haven't…"

"I have and it's yours forever and ever. *This* piano will never leave you."

I climbed over to him and fell on his chest. "Benjamin, you're the sweetest man alive. How am I so lucky to have you for my soul mate forever? Oh, Benjamin, let's get married tonight."

"Let's get out and see the piano," he said calmly. "Then we can plan our wedding, and quickly before you change your mind."

"I'll never change my mind. Never! Never! Never!"

We flew up the steps and into the music room. My mind seemed unable to take in what my eyes saw. "It's so beautiful. So big. And, oh Benjamin, you're such a darling. You got me a metronome to match the piano."

"The piano is of mahogany, a size larger than the one your father bought you, an M size. I was in luck that Mr. DeShazo had a metronome to match."

I sat down on the bench and began to play "Maria Elena." My eyes went to the glass walls and beyond. In the distance, lights from automobiles moved slowly toward Edisto Island. I thought about those people. I didn't know who they were, but I felt sympathy for them. No other woman had a man like Benjamin Bodicott. He always put others first and he had outdone himself in elevating me to a plateau from which I would never come down. I finished the tune and got up. "Benjamin, you've made me the happiest woman alive. How did I get so lucky as to have you for my life's mate? Let's be married as soon as we can arrange it."

"Would you like to be married in this house when it is finished?"

"Oh, yes. Yes! Let's be married here. Charlotte Ann will sit there at the piano and you and I will walk down the stairway at the back of the great hall, which will be filled with family and guests. I must tell Charlotte Ann about the wedding very soon. We'll have to select the pieces I want played at my wedding."

"There's one little detail..."

"What?"

"Lift the bench seat," he said.

I lifted the seat and there in the bench lay a diamond ring. When I grabbed it and held it before my eyes, the prisms of the chandelier and the diamonds reflected across the room. All was light and beauty. I handed the ring to Benjamin. "Would you do the honor?"

He slipped the ring on my finger and held me tight. I had the feeling of security and love a hundred times magnified. I held my hands over my head, in order to view the ring. Looking upward at my clasped hands and the diamonds, I realized a girl's hand never looks so good as when someone has slipped a diamond on it. It really was wonderful to wear an engagement ring. I'd never given much thought to it, but it was pure bliss. The dominant stone was large with smaller stones on each side. When I lowered my hand and let the ring reflect the light the sparkle was almost too bright to behold.

"The ring came from England," Benjamin said.

"England?"

"My mother's ring was from England and she loved it. I don't have my mother's ring but a jeweler in Savannah got this one. It's very much like hers. Do you really like it?"

"Oh my mercy. There aren't words to describe how much I love it. It's the symbol of our love and that will never change."

Benjamin looked a little anxious. "Darling," he whispered.

"Yes," I answered.

"I have a secret. When I disclose this to you, there will forever be nothing about me that is withheld from you."

Now I knew what he was coming to. What else could it be? "What is it?"

"When I was growing up on Corkery Island, no school boat was provided for me to go to the mainland and go to school. Whaley, I have never been to school."

"Shhh. I don't care about it, Benjamin. I *really* don't care. You're the brightest and most generous man alive. I wouldn't swap you for all the scholars at Harvard."

"I just wanted you to know…"

I put my fingers to his lips. "And I too have a secret," I revealed.

"Tell me. I will not speak of it."

"I don't like to talk about it, but I'm just going to say it. I don't want anyone to bring up the subject of the piano Daddy bought me. I don't know what Mother did with it and I don't want to know. Most of all, I don't want anyone to think the missing piano constitutes any restraint of our affections for each other. Perhaps she had a legitimate reason for whatever she did. Perhaps not. Some people would like nothing better than to latch on to this story and make a mess of it. Let's keep our secrets behind an unfound door."

"Forever and ever," Benjamin agreed.

Chapter Thirty

*B*enjamin and I held hands as we entered the door to the small white building bearing the banner "REUNION—CLASS OF 1951." Someone in a white dress hugged me. I pushed her back a little and recognized Pudgy, one of my best friends in high school. We hugged again and when I turned my head to look at somebody I smeared her white dress with lipstick. She flew away to remove the stain.

Millie Ann Moore's eyes indicated a blonde woman in a navy dress. "Whaley, do you know who *that* is?"

"No, who is it?" I asked as I watched a blonde beehive hairdo slowly making its way through a group of classmates.

"It's Jean Cannon."

"It cannot be. Jean Cannon was a string bean with black hair."

"That's Jean, believe it or not."

As though she could hear our voices, Jean turned and called, "Whaley McLeod. Where've you been, girl? I haven't seen you since graduation."

"You're the one who moved away," I said as I moved aside and indicated Benjamin. "This is my fiancé, Benjamin Bodicott. We're getting married in April."

"Benjamin, you're getting a girl who's good at math. She was the only one who could figure it out and had to help all the rest of us."

"Don't listen to her," I said.

"Are you the one who owns the Feed and Seed?" Jean asked at the very moment a young man turned me toward him and asked,

"Could this really be Whaley McLeod?"

"One and the same," I answered, trying my best to place him. "Arthur Fisher, whatever happened to you?" One thing that had happened was that his hair had turned white. Arthur introduced his wife, Lulu, and they told me about meeting each other at a restaurant in Charleston. I finally excused myself and found Benjamin surrounded by a group of gabbing girls asking about the wedding. He was trying to get out of the conversation but having little luck. I pulled him away and we found a chair at one of the tables set up for dining.

"I'm going to take you home early," I teased. "The girls are flirting with you."

He picked up my hand and my diamond flashed in the light. "I'm taken," he said.

Gwynn Knox finally came to a microphone and asked everyone to find a chair. He had some announcements to make. Two of my dearest school friends, Alicia and Elizabeth, sat near us, Alicia beside me and Elizabeth next to Benjamin. "Benjamin," she said, "I'm not going to apologize for leaning over you but I simply *must* talk to Whaley." She introduced her husband and I asked if they had children. "Only three," she laughed.

"You still giggle," I said. "You giggled so much I couldn't hear Miss Dunne."

"You did your part at giggling," she said.

Alicia had attended Coker College with me and we saw each other occasionally at college functions. She had gone on to graduate school in New England and gotten a plum of a job on the faculty at Davidson College. "I always knew you were the smartest girl in the class," I said.

"I'm not. I couldn't do math like you could."

"Your grades topped mine, always. How did you get that job at Davidson? Most people I know can't get admitted there as a student."

"It's a competitive college," she said. "I don't know how I made it. Just lucky I think."

"What do you teach?"

"I coach the debate team. And guess what. Do you remember Dr. Lineberger, the physician in Charleston?"

"Gosh, yes. All those shots he gave me? I'll never forget him."

"His grandson, Eban, is one of my students."

"He must be smart. Was Eban valedictorian?"

Alicia turned her head in amazement then turned back. "All of my students were valedictorians."

Benjamin had started a conversation with Alicia's husband, who held a degree in agriculture from Clemson. Harry asked Benjamin questions about feeds and seeds, which was just down his alley.

Before the plates were set down before us, I noticed some empty seats on the opposite side of the table. I whispered to Elizabeth that if no one sat there I just might help myself to a second glass of iced tea. Mine was nearly gone and the tea sitting at the empty spaces was tempting.

Gwynn continued to make announcements, but I didn't see anybody paying much attention to them. "We've lost one of our own," I heard him say, and perked up. "Junius Senn lost his life in an automobile accident. He leaves a widow and one child, but they were unable to attend tonight." Gwynn asked everyone in the room to bow their head for a minute in honor of Junius.

Gwynn then announced that dinner was about to be served. We would have a blessing and then visit with each other while we ate the meal. Afterward the members of the class of 1951 would gather for a picture, and we would dispend the activities of the evening by singing our school song. Grace was pronounced by Gwynn and just at that moment in flew the Middleton twins and their husbands. I could see they were still in the habit of dressing in identical outfits, this time in matching emerald green cocktail dresses with beaded clutch purses. Their eyes fell on the empty seats across from us.

"If the present arrivals sit across from us, I'm leaving," I whispered to Benjamin.

It was too late. They took seats and Callie was already leaning across the table making conversation with me. "I hear you two are getting married."

"That's right," I said, taking a bite of the steak that had been placed in front of me. "Who told you?"

"Your mother. Oh, Whaley, I think Mrs. McLeod is the nicest person in the world. I remember my own mother saying that I could visit your house anytime because your mother was such a nice lady."

Sallie got in on the conversation. "That's right. Mother always let us spend the night with you, Whaley, because she said your mother was a genteel lady."

"My, my," I said, mostly to Benjamin.

I gave close attention to Alicia and Elizabeth, trying to take up my time with them and ignore the Middleton twins. Benjamin seemed to be having a wonderful time talking with everyone. All the school chums were eyeing him. I didn't know if they realized I had made the catch of the century, but I knew it. I decided to flaunt my ring.

"Look at this," I said to Alicia, throwing my arm toward her. Some of my old friends got up and walked over to see the ring.

There was a lot of oooing and ahhing and I cast my arm toward Callie Middleton. "My engagement ring," I said.

Never in my entire life did I get the last word with Callie. Certainly not this time. She threw in her two cents' worth when she pulled my hand closer and turned it this way and the other and said how beautiful the ring was. I told her how very proud of it I was, and she lowered the boom. "Oh, Whaley, I've been meaning to ask you if you want the Shirmer music books. They don't mean much to me but you probably need them. They were in the piano bench and I just haven't packed them up and delivered them to you."

So. That is where the piano is. *In Callie Middleton's house.* Mother either sold it to her for a trifling sum or gave it to her outright.

For a minute I almost told her about my new Baldwin grand, but I let it go. I glanced at Benjamin to see whether he had heard Callie's remark. He was talking to a man about some new seeds that had arrived at the store. I pondered how I would handle this bombshell. Knowing Mother, she probably didn't know what she was doing to me. Music never meant much to her. She *was* appreciative of Callie and Sallie spending time with her after Daddy died. I had to admit that was a good gesture on their part.

"Do you want the Shirmer books?" Callie persisted. "I could drop them off at the Feed and Seed."

I reminded myself that I had a new piano, one much grander than Callie's. If I carried a grudge over the first Baldwin grand it would result in bitterness. I would weep and shed tears. There was no time for that. I had to handle it and right now. I would put it on the table and walk away from it forever. *Take care of it*, I nudged myself. "Callie, I have another Baldwin grand piano, and I've graduated from the Shirmer books. You can throw them away."

"I've never thrown a book away in my life," she answered.

"You can start with these." I didn't want to leave her on a sour note. I had to get rid of this thorn in my side tonight. If I didn't want to live with bitterness and jealousy in my soul I had to rise above my true feelings and forgive her and my mother. I had to do it now.

"You're angry," she said quietly.

"Not in the least. I feel better than I've felt in weeks. You have the piano and will make good use of it. I'm starting a new life with Benjamin, in a new home with a new piano. I'll not look backward, but forward. I wish you much happiness and joy as you play the piano." I turned to Benjamin. "I'm ready to go."

He got up and wished the best to those with whom he had talked. As he followed me out of the building, I said, "I just did something of honor, a task that brought great peace."

"What was it?"

"Something between old friends. I don't think others would understand. I want to go home to Charleston and have a nice quiet sleep. For once in my life, I did what I know is the right thing."

Chapter Thirty-one

All morning on the day of my wedding, I sang to no particular tune, "I'm getting married today." Julia, Hannah and I, taking special care of the wedding dress and cake, arrived at the new house at the same time the florist drove up. The florist and her helper hauled in ladders and got down to work trimming the stairway and big oval entrance to the great hall with garlands of greenery, smilax, orchids and camellias. She banked the piano in palm trees that reached high into the dome of the music room. That part of the house became a fairyland before our eyes. I had warned Benjamin about the bad luck said to accompany a bride and groom who see each other before the wedding. I didn't see him when I arrived so I quickly went upstairs and remained there, never getting a glimpse of him. There was a lot to do. My luggage was in the car, ready for the honeymoon trip, but I had to get into the wedding dress and veil. Time flew by.

Rather than arrive a minute too early for the nuptials, some of the guests drove their cars at a crawl on the long drive from the road to the house on the ridge. The house was especially beautiful from that driveway. As I got myself ready to walk down the steps, I didn't miss a thing. When I cracked the door I heard Jonny welcoming Mr. Lyon and some of the people I worked with at the courthouse. I heard Jonny call out, "Gift for the bride."

Benjamin and I had bought some furniture on King Street in Charleston and a few pieces in Savannah, but we barely had enough to make the house look like a home. Furniture is something

I cannot buy when I'm hurried and there was plenty of time to finish the house when we returned home from The Cloister. The red Dodge, with our luggage carefully tucked away, sat back from the house in a secluded nook of trees.

The preacher arrived and I ran to the door and cupped my ear. Jonny was placing him just right for his services. I ran back to the mirror for another look. Every hair was in place. The lace on my dress looked old but was new, just the way I wanted it. The dress was mid-length and had short sleeves. The Charleston dressmaker had fashioned lace gloves to match. My traveling outfit lay on the bed, ready for me to hop into after the service.

I stepped into the hallway but was afraid of being seen and backed into the room, cracking the door a bit so I could hear. Just then I heard the strains of Gounod's "Nocturne." I listened to every note and held my breath at the beauty of the piece. After that composition, Charlotte Ann began Debussy's "Clair de lune." That was my favorite piece in the whole world. Tears arose as I took in every note. It was played more beautifully at my wedding than ever before.

Jonny ran up the stairs. "The groom is ready to leave and meet you at the top of the stairway."

"How does he look?"

"Gorgeous. You won't know him. The white shirt and tie with a touch of red against the dark suit, shoes and socks, are perfect."

I ran to the dresser and picked up his ring. "Does he have my wedding band?"

"Oh, I'm sure. Absolutely. He wouldn't forget that."

"Let's go," Jonny said. "I'll run down quickly and in a minute, you follow me."

"Okay."

I gave my sister time to arrive in the great hall and slowly walked to the top of the steps. Mother looked so lovely. The orchid I had sent her was pinned to the French knot at the back of her head. I bit my lip and hoped I wouldn't cry.

Benjamin started up the stairs. He was heavenly. I reached for his arm as soon as he came to the top step. He looked at the Bible I was carrying and whispered, "The orchid is trembling."

"So am I," I said.

The Vanderhorst women, including Josephine, were behind me, keeping the train of my veil straight. We took each step slowly and deliberately. Charlotte Ann was playing the music I knew only as "Here Comes the Bride." When I reached the bottom step I smiled broadly at Mr. Lyon. Benjamin and I took baby steps as we walked to the high oval arch. It was so beautiful, with orchids placed in the green garlands and the last of the camellias from Benjamin's garden behind the Feed and Seed. Under the cascading flowers stood Dr. Spurgeon Goforth, the minister. Somewhere in the maze of flowers behind him I saw the countenance of Charlotte Ann's parents, Mr. and Mrs. Kell. We walked up to face the minister. He opened his book and began to read. Charlotte Ann was playing Handel's "Water Music."

I opened my mind to every word but didn't hear it. I was getting married and I wanted to take off my shoes and dance around the room. Hadn't Shakespeare written something about taking off one's shoes at a wedding? Never in my life had I been happier.

I calmed myself and heard Dr. Goforth say, "To have and to hold from this day forward, for better for worse, for richer for poorer, in sickness and in health, to love and to cherish, until death us do part."

He asked for the ring. Benjamin handed it to him. I extended my hand.

"With this ring I thee wed."

Benjamin was ever so graceful as I placed his ring on his finger. *We were married.*

"Those whom God hath joined together, let no man put asunder."

Just then Charlotte Ann hit the familiar notes that announce the marriage has been completed. Mr. Lyon flew over to me and said, "I'll be the first to kiss the bride." He gave me a fatherly kiss.

Benjamin was surrounded by my friends from the island. Cousin Mag and Cousin Shirley, from Jacksonville, hugged and kissed me. They had accompanied Mother on the trip to South Carolina.

"I'm going to the wedding cake," Julia said. "Don't forget, Whaley, that you get the first piece."

Benjamin and I eyed each other as we walked toward the dining room. We grinned. *We were married.*

I held the knife and his hand was over mine as the first piece was cut. I fed him a mouthful and he did the same for me. Mother took over the knife and began to serve the guests. She was graceful and poised. The orchid at the back of her head gave her a sort of class I'd never seen.

"I'm leaving now," I said to Benjamin. "I'm going to slip up to my room and get dressed. When I get to the car, I trust you'll be there."

Benjamin quickly left for the red Dodge.

Jonny handed me the orchid that had been on the Bible I had carried.

Within minutes I was wearing a beige suit, shoes and hat, all a perfect match, and flew down the steps. Benjamin helped me to the car. I quickly threw the orchid in the direction of the girls. Hannah caught it and Jonny and Julia made faces. Benjamin got in the car. He wasted no time getting the car back to the main road.

I gave a backward look. The story of Edisto Island seemed to flash before my eyes—the infinite marshes, the ospreys nesting in the cypress trees, the olive shells rolling ashore in the surf, the beads of sweat on the faces of the cotton pickers. That was the Edisto Island story. The story of Whaley McLeod Bodicott was just beginning.

End

About the Author

For almost twenty-five years Nancy and her husband Sid have traveled and explored the back roads and the people of coastal South Carolina and Georgia. Nancy has written twenty books focusing on the myth and history of the South. She has been awarded first-place prizes for ⟨...⟩f her books by a panel from ⟨...⟩niversity of South Carolina ⟨...⟩ge of Journalism. She has also ⟨...⟩cited for her work to promote ⟨...⟩y by speaking at over seventy-⟨...⟩ne residents of Myrtle Beach, ⟨...⟩a, South Carolina.

fiv⟨...⟩
N⟨...⟩